MW01405400

Washington University in St. Louis
St. Louis, Missouri

Written by Dan Carlin

*Edited by Adam Burns, Matt Hamman,
Kimberly Moore, and Jon Skindzier*

Layout by Meryl Sustarsic

*Additional contributions by Omid Gohari, Christina Koshzow,
Chris Mason, Joey Rahimi, and Luke Skurman*

ISBN # 1-4274-0214-0
ISSN # 1552-1583
© Copyright 2006 College Prowler
All Rights Reserved
Printed in the U.S.A.
www.collegeprowler.com

Last updated 5/09/08

Special Thanks To: Babs Carryer, Andy Hannah, LaunchCyte, Tim O'Brien, Bob Sehlinger, Thomas Emerson, Andrew Skurman, Barbara Skurman, Bert Mann, Dave Lehman, Daniel Fayock, Chris Babyak, The Donald H. Jones Center for Entrepreneurship, Terry Slease, Jerry McGinnis, Bill Ecenberger, Idie McGinty, Kyle Russell, Jacque Zaremba, Larry Winderbaum, Roland Allen, Jon Reider, Team Evankovich, Lauren Varacalli, Abu Noaman, Mark Exler, Daniel Steinmeyer, Jared Cohon, Gabriela Oates, David Koegler, and Glen Meakem.

Bounce-Back Team: Travis Petersen, Jess Minnen, and Matt Simonton

College Prowler®
5001 Baum Blvd.
Suite 750
Pittsburgh, PA 15213

Phone: 1-800-290-2682
Fax: 1-800-772-4972
E-Mail: info@collegeprowler.com
Web Site: www.collegeprowler.com

College Prowler® is not sponsored by, affiliated with, or approved by Washington University in St. Louis in any way.

College Prowler® strives faithfully to record its sources. As the reader understands, opinions, impressions, and experiences are necessarily personal and unique. Accordingly, there are, and can be, no guarantees of future satisfaction extended to the reader.

© Copyright 2006 College Prowler. All rights reserved. No part of this work may be reproduced or transmitted in any form or by any means, including but not limited to, photocopy, recording, or any information storage and retrieval systems, without the express written permission of College Prowler®.

How this all started...

When I was trying to find the perfect college, I used every resource that was available to me. I went online to visit school websites; I talked with my high school guidance counselor; I read book after book; I hired a private counselor. Sure, this was all very helpful, but nothing really told me what life was like at the schools I cared about. These sources weren't giving me enough information to be totally confident in my decision.

In all my research, there were only two ways to get the information I wanted.

The first was to physically visit the campuses and see if things were really how the brochures described them, but this was quite expensive and not always feasible. The second involved a missing ingredient: the students. Actually talking to a few students at those schools gave me a taste of the information that I needed so badly. The problem was that I wanted more but didn't have access to enough people.

In the end, I weighed my options and decided on a school that felt right and had a great academic reputation, but truth be told, the choice was still very much a crapshoot. I had done as much research as any other student, but was I 100 percent positive that I had picked the school of my dreams?

Absolutely not.

My dream in creating *College Prowler* was to build a resource that people can use with confidence. My own college search experience taught me the importance of gaining true insider insight; that's why the majority of this guide is composed of quotes from actual students. After all, shouldn't you hear about a school from the people who know it best?

I hope you enjoy reading this book as much as I've enjoyed putting it together. Tell me what you think when you get a chance. I'd love to hear your college selection stories.

Luke Skurman
CEO and Co-Founder
lukeskurman@collegeprowler.com

Welcome to College Prowler®

During the writing of College Prowler's guidebooks, we felt it was critical that our content was unbiased and unaffiliated with any college or university. We think it's important that our readers get honest information and a realistic impression of the student opinions on any campus—that's why if any aspect of a particular school is terrible, we (unlike a campus brochure) intend to publish it. While we do keep an eye out for the occasional extremist—the cheerleader or the cynic—we take pride in letting the students tell it like it is. We strive to create a book that's as representative as possible of each particular campus. Our books cover both the good and the bad, and whether the survey responses point to recurring trends or a variation in opinion, these sentiments are directly and proportionally expressed through our guides.

College Prowler guidebooks are in the hands of students throughout the entire process of their creation. Because you can't make student-written guides without the students, we have students at each campus who help write, randomly survey their peers, edit, layout, and perform accuracy checks on every book that we publish. From the very beginning, student writers gather the most up-to-date stats, facts, and inside information on their colleges. They fill each section with student quotes and summarize the findings in editorial reviews. In addition, each school receives a collection of letter grades (A through F) that reflect student opinion and help to represent contentment, prominence, or satisfaction for each of our 20 specific categories. Just as in grade school, the higher the mark the more content, more prominent, or more satisfied the students are with the particular category.

Once a book is written, additional students serve as editors and check for accuracy even more extensively. Our bounce-back team—a group of randomly selected students who have no involvement with the project—are asked to read over the material in order to help ensure that the book accurately expresses every aspect of the university and its students. This same process is applied to the 200-plus schools College Prowler currently covers. Each book is the result of endless student contributions, hundreds of pages of research and writing, and countless hours of hard work. All of this has led to the creation of a student information network that stretches across the nation to every school that we cover. It's no easy accomplishment, but it's the reason that our guides are such a great resource.

When reading our books and looking at our grades, keep in mind that every college is different and that the students who make up each school are not uniform—as a result, it is important to assess schools on a case-by-case basis. Because it's impossible to summarize an entire school with a single number or description, each book provides a dialogue, not a decision, that's made up of 20 different topics and hundreds of student quotes. In the end, we hope that this guide will serve as a valuable tool in your college selection process. Enjoy!

OMID GOHARI ○ CHRISTINA KOSHZOW ○ CHRIS MASON ○ JOEY RAHIMI ○ LUKE SKURMAN ○
The College Prowler Team

WASHINGTON UNIVERSITY IN ST. LOUIS
Table of Contents

By the Numbers............................ **1**	Drug Scene.............................. **102**
Academics **4**	Campus Strictness **107**
Local Atmosphere **11**	Parking...................................... **112**
Safety & Security **18**	Transportation **117**
Computers.................................. **23**	Weather.................................... **123**
Facilities...................................... **28**	Report Card Summary **127**
Campus Dining.......................... **34**	Overall Experience **128**
Off-Campus Dining **41**	The Inside Scoop..................... **132**
Campus Housing **50**	Finding a Job or Internship **138**
Off-Campus Housing................. **63**	Alumni **140**
Diversity..................................... **69**	Student Organizations............ **142**
Guys & Girls............................... **74**	The Best & Worst..................... **145**
Athletics..................................... **80**	Visiting...................................... **147**
Nightlife..................................... **87**	Words to Know........................ **152**
Greek Life **96**	

Introduction from the Author

There is a joke at Washington University, grown a bit old through repetition, about the University's generic name. Ask twenty people on the street where to look for Washington University, half will describe a sprawling state college, basking on the West Coast (they're thinking of the University of Washington, in Seattle). The other half will tell you that it's an institute of political science, located in our nation's capital (they're thinking of George Washington University).

Washington University in St. Louis has fought an uphill battle to achieve name recognition as a top university. But after hosting 2004 presidential debates, graduating Rhodes Scholars and a *Real World* cast member (Cara Nussbaum, '01), playing a central role in the Human Genome Project, and ascending to a place among America's best colleges, Wash U has overcome its relative obscurity. It now competes for America's most accomplished high school seniors, alongside the colleges of the Ivy League.

Like the typical Midwestern city that it inhabits, Wash U straddles the line between provincial and cosmopolitan, liberal and conservative. It's a school known for working its students hard in class, but rewarding them with a lax, party atmosphere. Its classically beautiful campus, which recalls Princeton University's Gothic distinction, contradicts Wash U's relative youth (established as a Unitarian seminary in 1853 by the family of T.S. Eliot, it was a day school until the 1960s). Wash U is, above all else, an institution in full development, architecturally and temperamentally. A lack of hallowed traditions means that students can constantly invent their own.

For an increasing number of high school seniors, then, Wash U has become an attractive place to spend four years. It has its quirks and drawbacks, as well, which this guide will point out. By giving you a detailed and unbiased look at student life at Washington University, I hope this volume will make your choice of college easier, and render your decision a more informed and successful one.

Dan Carlin, Author
Washington University in St. Louis

By the Numbers

General Information

Washington University
1 Brookings Drive
St. Louis, MO 63130

Control:
Private

Academic Calendar:
Semester

Religious Affiliation:
None

Founded:
1853

Web Site:
www.wustl.edu

Main Phone:
(314) 935-5000

Student Body

Full-Time Undergraduates:
7,181

Part-Time Undergraduates:
72

Total Male Undergraduates:
3,699

Total Female Undergraduates:
3,554

Admissions

Overall Acceptance Rate:
17%

Early Decision Acceptance Rate:
N/A

Early Action Acceptance Rate:
Not offered

Regular Acceptance Rate:
17%

Total Applicants:
22,428

Total Acceptances:
3,813

Freshman Enrollment:
1,338

Yield (% of admitted students who actually enroll):
35%

Early Decision Deadline:
November 15

Early Decision Notification:
December 15

Regular Decision Deadline:
January 15

Regular Decision Notification:
April 1

Must-Reply-By Date:
May 1

Students Enrolled from Waiting List:
134

Transfer Applications Received:
1,030

Transfer Applicants Offered Admission:
214

Transfer Applicants Enrolled:
214

SAT I or ACT Required?
Yes, either

SAT I Range (25th–75th Percentile):
1370–1530

SAT I Verbal Range (25th–75th Percentile):
680–750

SAT I Math Range (25th–75th Percentile):
690–780

ACT Composite Range (25th–75th Percentile):
30–33

Retention Rate:
97%

Top 10% of High School Class:
93%

Common Application Accepted?
Yes

Supplemental Forms?
Yes

Application Fee:
$55

Admissions Phone:
(800) 638-0700

Admissions E-Mail:
admissions@wustl.edu

Admissions Web Site:
admissions.wustl.edu

Financial Information

Tuition:
$36,200

Room and Board:
$11,636

Books and Supplies:
$1,220

Average Need-Based Financial Aid Package (including loans, work-study, grants, and other sources):
$29,491

Students Who Applied for Financial Aid:
71%

Applicants Who Received Aid:
55%

Financial Aid Forms Deadline:
February 15

Financial Aid Phone:
(888) 547-6670

Financial Aid Web Site:
sfs.wustl.edu

Financial Aid E-Mail:
financial@wustl.edu

Academics

The Lowdown On...
Academics

Degrees Awarded:
Bachelor's
Master's
Doctorate
First professional

Most Popular Majors:
17% Social sciences
14% Business/marketing
13% Engineering
10% Psychology
10% Visual/performing arts

Undergraduate Schools:
College of Arts & Sciences
George Warren Brown School of Social Work
Olin School of Business
Sam Fox School of Design & Visual Arts
School of Engineering

Full-time Faculty:
838

Faculty with Terminal Degree:
99%

Student-to-Faculty Ratio:
7:1

Average Course Load:
5 courses

Graduation Rates:
Four Year: 83%
Five Year: 91%
Six Year: 92%

Special Degree Options

Accelerated degree program, adult/continuing education programs, advanced placement credit, cross-registration, double major, English as a Second Language (ESL), exchange student program (domestic), independent study, internships, liberal arts/career combination, student-designed major, study abroad, teacher certificate program

AP Test Score Requirements

Possible credit for scores of 4 or 5

IB Test Score Requirements

Possible credit for scores of 6 or 7

Best Places to Study

Brown Library, Ursa's Café, Holmes Lounge, and the Law School Library

Sample Academic Clubs

American Institute of Chemical Engineers (AIChE), Association for Computing Machinery (ACM), Black Pre-Law Society (BPL), Philosophia, Pre-Medical Society, Washington University Academic Team (WUAT), Washington University Debate Team

Did You Know?

In 2000, Washington University hosted the **presidential debates** between George W. Bush and Al Gore, and in 2004, the debates between George W. Bush and John Kerry.

Students Speak Out On...
Academics

> "The teachers are fine. Freshmen classes are mostly lectures, but all of the professors I've had interactions with have been pretty approachable."

Q "There are really some exceptional professors—as opposed to just good scholars—at Wash U. The political science department has a few great teachers, especially Prof Mertha (his courses on Chinese politics are excellent) and Prof Rehfeld. In other areas, Richard Smith teaches a terrific intro course on human evolution, virtually any course with Prof Koepnick (German film and media studies department) is interesting, and Prof Symeonoglu's intro archeology/art history course, Myths and Monuments of Antiquity, is a must. However, **it's really key to shop around in the first week-and-a-half of classes before sticking with a set of courses**. There are so many to choose from, and it's easy to miss the best ones!"

Q "The professors I've had at Wash U have been good overall. There are **those ones who are painfully boring**, but not too many. All the professors are very accessible outside of class, and they like it when you come in to talk to them. So far, all the professors I've had have been great with answering questions and helping me out and stuff."

Q "Whether or not you have a good academic experience at Wash U **depends on the department**. Most of the professors I've had have been decent. There are always a few bad apples, but in general it's been a good experience for me."

Q "There are some amazing professors, and the inevitable crappy ones (which you can often avoid by finding out about them before taking the class). The 100-level computer science class I took first semester was taught by this amazing professor . . . He was extremely nice and easy to follow. One thing I found about a lot of professors is that **they truly care about the students**. From what I've heard about other universities, this is definitely not always the case."

Q "**Some teachers here are fantastic**! Depends on the class really—also, they're really great about giving teachers and not TAs (teaching assistants). The only class you'll have that will be taught by a TA will be your English Composition class your freshman year. Especially awesome teachers that everyone knows and loves: Richard Smith (he teaches Intro to Evolution and is apparently phenomenal), I've also loved Prof Bernard (physics teacher who moves discussions at a nice, steady pace), Prof Friedman (history and women's studies; probably the best woman teacher here), Prof Huck (teaches art school, mostly printmaking, and has a knack for the arts), Prof Sabraw (teaches art school, mostly drawing, and will work tirelessly with each individual student), and John Stewart (the chorus director who is also a phenomenal human being)."

Q "Your academic experience here depends on which teachers you have. I loved all of mine except for one. It depends on your major and who you get. When you know what classes you want to take, **I absolutely recommend asking someone who's in your major who you should take**. It can make a huge difference, even with the same class."

Q "The professors are generally **very interested in their students**. They are also accessible outside of class—I think teachers are required to have a few hours per week of open hours to see students. You can also make an appointment with your professors over e-mail and they are more than happy to meet with you."

Q "The women's studies department, the legal studies department, the film and media studies department, the English and writing department, and the pre-law department are full of really great people. **I've never had a problem with any professor, though, in any department**. All teachers are very willing to help and interested in your work and your learning. I'm beginning an independent thesis project for next semester jointly with the women's studies department, the music department, and the film and media studies department, because all of the professors I approached were interested in my proposal and assured me that I wouldn't be working alone. So that's an example of their cooperation and willingness to work together for their students. It's been really great so far. Oh, and FYI, the writing professors are phenomenal."

Q "The teachers here are **absolutely amazing**! Not only do they really know their class material and try to make it interesting, which is especially important in potentially dry classes like Accounting and Finance, they are also incredibly nice and approachable. Professors also really go out of their way to get to know you and help you. I've had professors help me with problems in course material from other classes, revise my resume, help me find a job, and much more.

Q "All of the professors I have had have been great. Teachers are totally willing to help you and are always encouraging you to come by if you have a question or just to say 'hi.' **Teachers simply want to get to know you**. I've gotten to know professors and administrators very well through my classes and through my involvement on campus."

The College Prowler Take On...
Academics

Most Wash U students seem to enjoy their academic experience and have a good relationship with their teachers. There are certainly boring and exciting courses and professors in each department, so it's recommended both to ask for advice from older students and to visit multiple classes before settling on a schedule. The professors seem particularly notable for their enthusiasm in receiving visits from students during or beyond office hours. Those who have made an effort to seek help and advice from them are usually rewarded with genuine interest, help with school work, and future recommendations.

The University's reputation has rested principally on its achievements in the sciences, but most departments—from English to women's studies and psychology—are now very strong. Within the different undergraduate schools there are more noticeable disparities. The Olin School of Business, for example, allegedly has a weak faculty compared to that of the college of arts and sciences. While students aren't usually overwhelmed with their course work, academics are rigorous in all of the undergraduate schools of Wash U—although among all undergrads, pre-meds seem the most perpetually stressed. The curricula in several of the schools include distribution requirements, recently organized into a cluster system, but there are also opportunities for designing more creative programs of study: individualized majors, cross-disciplinary courses, and independent projects all allow students to pursue their interests without being limited to traditional subject areas.

The College Prowler® Grade on
Academics: A-

A high Academics grade generally indicates that professors are knowledgeable, accessible, and genuinely interested in their students' welfare. Other determining factors include class size, how well professors communicate, and whether or not classes are engaging.

Local Atmosphere

The Lowdown On...
Local Atmosphere

Region:
Midwest

City, State:
St. Louis, MO

Setting:
Medium-sized city

Distance from Chicago:
4 hours

Distance from Columbia:
2 hours

Distance from Kansas City:
3 hours

Points of Interest:
Riverside casinos, the city museum, the Arch

Closest Movie Theaters:

The Esquire
6706 Clayton Rd.
Phone: (314) 542-4AMC

The Hi-Pointe
Skinker and Clayton Rd.
Phone: (314) 995-6273

The Tivoli
6350 Delmar Blvd.
Phone: (314) 995-6270

Major Sports Teams:

Blues (hockey)
Cardinals (baseball)
Rams (football)

City Web Site

stlouis.missouri.org

Did You Know?

Five Fun Facts about St. Louis:

- **Blues music is big in St. Louis**. Every year, there are several large festivals, such as the Muddy Blues and Roots Festivals, the Ribs and Blues Festivals, and others.
- St. Louis has the **biggest Bosnian immigrant population** in the country.
- In 1904, St. Louis was host to the World's Fair, and to the **first Olympic Games** to take place in the United States.
- Every month, owner Joe Edwards changes the window display at **Blueberry Hill**, a popular bar/restaurant in the Loop.
- **Most famous people who were born here left** as soon as they could (see famous St. Louisans list).

Famous St. Louisans:

Chuck Berry, Bob Costas, Miles Davis, T.S. Eliot, Jonathan Franzen, Ron Isley, Albert King, Clark Terry

Local Slang:

The Landing – A plaza of bars and nightclubs located next to the Mississippi River.

Scurred – Afraid.

The Lou – A familiar term for St. Louis.

East Side – The seedy towns across the Mississippi River known for their casinos and strip clubs.

The Loop – The commercial area around Delmar Boulevard in University City.

Students Speak Out On...
Local Atmosphere

"St. Louis is an amazing town. Wash U is located in a relatively suburban area just minutes away from downtown, so you have access to all the clubs and restaurants of a big city, without the traffic and pollution."

Q "The big Missouri state school, Mizzou, is in Columbia, about an hour and 45 minutes away. The good thing about that is if a band is coming through town and they missed St. Louis for some reason, sometimes they stop in Columbia. Ani Difranco is known for playing in STL, then the next night in Columbia. That gets crazy. **Webster University (in Webster Groves) usually has a ton of cool things going on**—from drag shows to plays and films. It's a huge visual arts/film school, so there's tons of stuff to do there. I don't know if you're into sports, but St. Louis basically supports itself on the St. Louis Cardinals, the Rams, and the Blues. The city would be dead without them. Wineries are a big thing, too, outside of St. Louis, and that's always fun."

Q "St. Louis is a really great place to live. **Stay away from East St. Louis (it's across the river so you'd never be there anyway)**. The Loop is an awesome area. It's a 10-minute walk north of campus with really kick-ass restaurants, shopping, stores, etc."

Q "There are **some cool things to see here**: the St. Louis Arch, the Budweiser Brewery, the art museum, the zoo, and much more. There really isn't too much of an area I would avoid . . . with the exception of East St. Louis, but that is in Illinois."

Q "**St. Louis is known for the Arch**, although I have yet to ride up the Arch. Overall, the atmosphere is pretty nice. I come from Miami where people are pretty mean . . . St. Louis is nothing at all what I was used to. Everyone here is really nice."

Q "I love the atmosphere in STL. **It's nice to be in a city, but not a huge metropolis**. There are lots of other universities in the St. Louis area, so it's a pretty young city too. The zoo in STL is really cool, and it's free. It's also really close to campus—you could even walk there. I love it."

Q "A lot of Wash U students come from New York City and other big East Coast cities, and they don't rag on St. Louis too much, so it can't be that bad. Actually, most students just stay on campus, and don't really get out, so they don't know what's out there. **There are actually plenty of things to do, beyond the ordinary attractions** (Arch, zoo, art museum, etc.). There are some great, lesser-known bars like the Venice Café or the Upstairs Lounge, weird shopping districts like Cherokee Street (it's all retro clothing/furniture stores and antique shops), and cool ethnic neighborhoods like South Grand. Of course, the Loop is nearby, and it's an old leftist/hippy strip that's become a little more commercial in recent years, but it still has a laid-back atmosphere and there are a couple of cool bars and cafés."

Q "St. Louis is not really a college town, but **there's a lot of fun free stuff to do in Forest Park**, which is nearby, like the zoo or art museum; and the Loop is a neighborhood near school, which is fun. There's also a cool concert venue called the Pageant within walking distance"

Q "Webster University and St. Louis University are both in town, but **most students tend to stay in and around their own campuses**."

Q "We are in a gorgeous and pretty wealthy area of St. Louis—it's really lovely. There's a university right next to ours, Fontbonne, but no one has ever seen the students there (it's sort of an on-going WU joke that no one actually attends Fontbonne). There's also Webster and SLU, but **we at Wash U don't usually interact with students from those schools** very much.

Q "**I sometimes feel like I never get off campus**. We're located in a great place, and in a really nice part of town. There are other universities around, such as St. Louis University, University of Missouri, St. Louis, Fontbonne University (just across the street), and Webster University. We have one big mixer with all the other universities in the fall, so there's a chance to meet other students.

Q "I wouldn't say there's anything to stay away from, but **definitely take advantage of downtown St. Louis**. The Arch is a must see, and Union Station has good food and shopping. The Galleria is really close, and we're really close to Forest Park (Wash U is right next to it, actually) which has a bunch of things to see for free: the art museum, a history museum, science center, and much more."

Q "There are several other universities in St. Louis: **Saint Louis University (cute guys)**, Webster, and many others. So once you're able to venture off campus, you can meet a lot of interesting people. Also, there are lots of fun places to visit, especially Forest Park which is actually right by campus. They have everything: a zoo, museums, science center, great places to walk or run; it's just really nice. If you visit Wash U's Web site (*www.wustl.edu*) and click on the "Visitors & the St. Louis Area" link, it will tell you lots of things to do and see here!"

The College Prowler Take On...
Local Atmosphere

The atmosphere in St. Louis is not one of a traditional college town, as most students agree. The city is big enough that kids feel they can get away and find the resources of a semi-metropolis. At the same time, the campus is in a calm suburb, where there is a laid-back Midwestern atmosphere that many students from the East Coast find appealing. The immediate area surrounding the campus also offers plenty of fun opportunities: Forest Park to the east has a 10K bike trail, an 18-hole golf course, tennis courts, the world-class Saint Louis Art Museum, gondola-equipped lakes, and plenty of picnic grounds. The Loop is a commercial district bordering campus on the north, with plenty of cafés, bars, shops, restaurants, a nice movie theater, and a few music venues. Most students seem to stay in the general area of campus, but there are also many things to do downtown and throughout the metro area.

The city seems to be on a slow and steady upswing. Washington Avenue houses a strip of trendy, hip bars and nightclubs, worth at least a weekend–evening visit. There are also neat little areas stashed around town that take a little digging to discover, like the cool stores on South Grand Boulevard, the bars on Pestalozzi Avenue, and the vibrant African American neighborhoods in North St. Louis. The main problem with St. Louis for students seems to be its lack of centrality. Attractions are spread out all over the metro area, making it difficult to see everything in one outing, and rendering exploration difficult without a car. The construction of Metrolink stations (the St. Louis elevated train line) next to campus, however, should improve accessibility.

The College Prowler® Grade on Local Atmosphere: B+

A high Local Atmosphere grade indicates that the area surrounding campus is safe and scenic. Other factors include nearby attractions, proximity to other schools, and the town's attitude toward students.

Safety & Security

The Lowdown On...
Safety & Security

Number of Wash U Police:
40, 26 of which are deputized police officers

Phone:
(314) 935-5555 (emergencies)
(314) 935-5533 (non-emergencies)

Safety Services:
24-hour emergency response devices and patrol

Controlled dormitory access

Late-night transport/escort service

RAD self-defense program

STOP tag system to prevent computer theft

Student patrols

Health Center:

4525 Scott Ave.
Room 3420, East Building

(314) 935-6666

Hours: Monday–Thursday
8 a.m.–6 p.m.,
Friday 8 a.m.–5 p.m, Saturday–Sunday 10 a.m.–2 p.m.;
Urgent Care Services: Monday–Friday 5 p.m.–11 p.m.

Health Services:

Basic medical services

Counseling and psychiatric services

On-site pharmaceuticals

STD screening

Did You Know?

St. Louis's proximity to the New Madrid fault line means that earthquakes can happen at Washington University. Minor tremors are more likely than a severe earthquake; nonetheless, you should take precautions and prepare in advance.

Students Speak Out On...
Safety & Security

> "Security on campus is great. We have blue-light emergency phones all over campus. There are also always officers on patrol, and they have a number you can call if you want an escort or a ride."

Q "Safety on campus is pretty good. **There are blue-light emergency phones everywhere**, you need a card to get into any of the dorm buildings (so there's no way for strangers to wander in), there are proctors stationed in the lobbies of all buildings open at night, and there are constantly campus police patrolling. The school also has a service for people who don't want to walk across campus alone; you can call the number and two guys who work for the service will show up wherever you are and walk with you so you don't have to be by yourself."

Q "**North of the school is a rather sketchy area**, and occasionally weird people will wander from their neighborhood and onto campus. There have been a few incidents, but as far as I am aware, nothing severe. I walk around campus by myself at night all the time, and I've never had a problem."

Q "As a girl, **I've never felt unsafe** walking around campus day or night. If you are afraid, you usually just find people to walk with you. No biggie."

Q "The Wash U campus is in a **very nice neighborhood**. Most students feel safe walking around. We have a visible police force and emergency phones everywhere you look. The only crime you really ever hear of is petty theft."

Q "Campus safety is really great; I've never felt unsafe. The Wash U campus is so small that **you're never really very far from people who can help if you do have a problem**. You also have to have a student ID to get into any of the dorms because you use it to deactivate the locks."

Q "I have never felt unsafe on campus. If you're at the library or the art school finishing a project at 2 a.m., you can call the campus police and they'd be more than happy to have **an escort take you back to the dorm** (free, of course)."

Q "I have never felt unsafe on campus. **There are police patrolling the campus at all hours**, blue-light security phones all over the place, and the campus is pretty well lit. If you ever don't feel safe, you can call for an escort, and they'll come and pick you up from wherever you are and take you home. Of course, the escorts don't always come immediately after you call them. I once waited for over an hour."

Q "Security at Wash U is okay. We have a police force, night escorts, and night shuttles and buses. I've never had to use them. There are also bike cops that patrol the off-campus housing areas. I'm not going to lie, though, I don't usually go anywhere by myself, and I try to get off campus before it gets too late. **Random things do happen here**."

Q "Personally, I have never had any problems. Walking around on campus at night has never been an issue for me. I always feel safe."

The College Prowler Take On...
Safety & Security

Whatever crimes occur at Wash U invariably show up in the "Police Beat" section of *Student Life*, the main student newspaper. There are often detailed reports about "green, leafy substances" being confiscated from unlucky students, stolen bottles of tequila, and other minor incidents, but overwhelmingly, there is little crime, and little reason to feel unsafe at Wash U. The campus is nestled between three upscale neighborhoods, making it a safe place to live and study. None of those interviewed could recall an instance in which he or she felt threatened or unsafe on campus.

The presence of campus police and blue-light security phones make most students feel perfectly at ease, and since most areas of the campus are well lit and usually frequented, walking around campus late at night doesn't make many students nervous. Of course, no campus can completely protect students from one another, and instances of date rape and assault have been reported in recent years, but the University provides self-defense courses to help prevent rape or date rape from occurring.

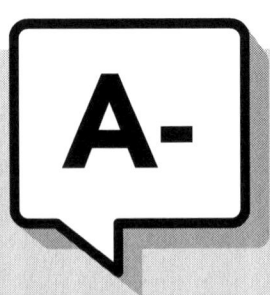

The College Prowler® Grade on

Safety & Security: A-

A high grade in Safety & Security means that students generally feel safe, campus police are visible, blue-light phones and escort services are readily available, and safety precautions are not overly necessary.

Computers

The Lowdown On...
Computers

High-Speed Network?
Yes

Wireless Network?
Yes

Number of Labs:
7, plus 11 residence hall labs for any students living on campus and their visitors.

Number of Computers:
2,500

Operating Systems:
Mac
PC
UNIX

Free Software
Ad-Aware, Norton AntiVirus, and Spybot

Discounted Software
None

24-Hour Labs
Located in all dorms in the South 40 (the primary on-campus residence halls), the Village, Frat Row, and Millbrook, Rosedale, and Greenway Apartments.

Charge to Print?
No

Did You Know?

Students can purchase **discounted computers through the University**. Call the Student Technology Resource and Support Services (STaRS) at (314) 935-7100 for more information.

Students Speak Out On...
Computers

"Most people at Wash U have their own computers. There are Ethernet connections in most of the dorm rooms, and each dorm has its own computer lab. Whenever I have had to use a lab computer, I've never had trouble finding an open one."

Q "It's not entirely necessary, but **it's certainly useful to have a personal computer with you**. The Ethernet network is fast enough for most things, but file-sharing has become kind of a pain. The network is programmed to limit download speeds from off-campus servers, so a lot of programs are very slow. There are on-campus trading networks, though, so it's easy to give and receive movie and music files."

Q "The school network is fine. The **computer labs usually aren't that crowded** because most people do have their own computers. You don't need a computer, but it is a really nice thing to have for functions like AIM and computer games. Also, if you plan on having a writing-intensive major, it is a nice thing to have one in your room."

Q "It would be nice to have your own computer, if possible, but it's not a necessity. **Almost all of the dorms have a computer lab inside, so you don't have to walk far**. There are computer labs all around campus available to students, so it should not be a problem to find a computer should you choose not to bring one."

Q "The computer **labs are generally always open**. The labs on main campus close around midnight–1 a.m., but there are computer labs at the bottom of the dorms that are open 24 hours. You don't have to bring your own computer, but I found it very helpful to have my own. I just brought a laptop, and I didn't get a printer."

Q "Everyone gets a Wash U e-mail address, and you can be connected from your dorm room. There are computer labs throughout campus, but they tend to be crowded during certain times of day. **I found it more convenient to have one in my room**, but there are plenty of people without their own computers and they manage fine without one. Most of the dorms have small computer centers in them as well."

The College Prowler Take On...
Computers

Even though Wash U isn't the most wired campus in the country (compared to, say, Carnegie Mellon University or MIT), it has all of the basic resources: an Ethernet network, computer labs, printers, and file-sharing programs. Ethernet jacks and Wi-Fi capabilities have been installed all over campus, so laptop users should have no problems getting connected. Most students do bring their own computers, even though many say that it isn't indispensable. Since most dorms have 24-hour computer labs and there are 2,500 computers on campus, there is almost always one available when you need it.

When deciding whether to bring a computer or not, it's useful to consider your subject area. For more writing-intensive majors such as English and political science, it can be convenient to be able to type your papers outside of a lab. For biology and chemistry, you won't need the service of a printer as much. Laptops will be more and more useful as the campus becomes more wireless-friendly, and desktops can be a real pain in an already-cramped dorm room. A note on computer facilities: the most commonly-used labs on Wash U's campus are the arts and sciences computing lab in Eads Hall, and the computer room in Olin Library. However, there are plenty of computers in less frequented and more pleasant spots, like the Social Sciences Computing Facility (SSCF), which enjoys a broad-window view onto campus from Eliot Hall, or the lab in the beautiful G.W. Brown School of Social Work Library.

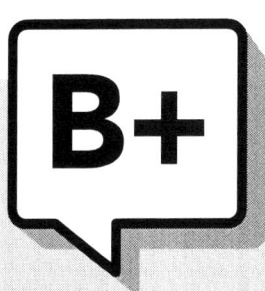

The College Prowler® Grade on
Computers: B+

A high grade in Computers designates that computer labs are available, the computer network is easily accessible, and the campus' computing technology is up-to-date.

Facilities

The Lowdown On...
Facilities

Student Center:
Mallinckrodt is the current student center, and the massive, newly planned University Center is projected to be finished in 2009.

Athletic Center:
The athletic complex (the AC)

Popular Places to Chill:
Bowles Plaza, the Quad, Ursa's

Campus Size:
169 acres

Favorite Things to Do:
You can play Frisbee golf around campus, climb trees next to the art school, or check out student concerts in Graham Chapel.

What Is There to Do on Campus?

You can go for a swim in the AC, listen to CDs while you study in one of the music library's listening rooms, catch a play in Edison Theater, or check out a hip-hop battle at the Gargoyle.

Movie Theater on Campus?

Not exactly, but there's a big screen in the huge lecture hall, Brown 100, where the film and media studies courses hold their screenings. The campus film series, Filmboard, uses the Galleria 6 cinemas at an off-campus mall.

Bowling on Campus?

No

Bar on Campus?

No, the Rathskeller used to serve beer on tap, but was converted into a Subway sandwich shop. The new University Center is tentatively planning a restaurant that may serve alcohol, though this remains uncertain.

Coffeehouse on Campus?

Yes, the Hilltop Café on main campus, and Ursa's on the South 40.

Libraries

Art & Architecture (Steinberg Hall), Biology (Life Sciences Building, Room 200), Business (Simon, 290), Chemistry (Louderman, 549), Earth & Planetary Sciences (Wilson, 214), East Asian (January, 209), Law (Anheuser Busch Hall), Mathematics (Cupples I, 016), Medicine (660 S Euclid, Medical School), Music (Gaylord), John Olin (main library, center of campus), Physics (Compton, 340), Social Work (Brown, 300), and West Campus (7425, Forsyth, lower level)

Students Speak Out On...
Facilities

"Some departments have nicer buildings than others. The physics department building is still stuck in the '60s, just like the faculty. The athletic facilities also leave something to be desired."

"**The weight room is a joke**. The machines are very old and break down a lot, and the room is too small. It's definitely not adequate for the needs of the undergraduate and graduate students. And the other sports equipment isn't great either. If you want to borrow a badminton net, it will probably have holes in it. The basketballs are probably lopsided!"

"The athletic center is really nice. **There are tons of facilities that you can use there**, like the racquetball courts, the weight room, a gym, basketball courts, and lots of other things. The computer labs are nice, too. They have both Macs and PCs, so you can use whatever you're more comfortable with. I haven't really used the student center much, just the bookstore, really, but it's pretty nice from what I've heard. The administration and the student-run organizations plan a lot of cool things for us, like parties (yes, they have beer there) and things like that."

"Athletic facilities are pretty good here. We have a pool, two gyms, a track, and athletic fields and stuff. Computers here are fine. There are zillions around and on campus. There are labs in every dorm, as well as a huge art-sci computing lab on main campus. I don't know if we really have a student center, per se, but **there are many places to chill on campus**. Life is just fine at Wash U."

Q "At this point, Wash U tends to be focused on the basics in terms of facilities: **classroom buildings with no architectural distinction, limited computer access, shabby cafeterias**. So it tends to neglect the finer things, like game rooms, music venues, practice rooms, and athletic facilities—which all exist on campus, but aren't necessarily brand-new or top-of-the-line. Generally, if you want to do something on or off campus, it's possible to do it. And they did recently renovate the library. Another great resource is the campus rock music club, the Gargoyle. On Wednesdays and Thursdays it presents groups like Deep Banana Blackout and Yonder Mountain String Band, and even comedians in the basement of Mallinckrodt Center. Mitch Hedberg came before he died. Lots of things, like the student center and the main library, have recently been under construction, though, so facilities are probably going to improve in the future."

Q "The student center on campus is Mallinckrodt, which has the food court, an area called the Gargoyle which serves as extra seating during lunch time (and, I think, has vegetarian and Kosher food counters). **At night, the Gargoyle houses small concerts (there's a stage), and Vanilla Ice came a few years ago**! I don't think that one was very well attended. There are also parties and fun events, like talents shows, lip sync contests, and much more. Mallinckrodt also houses a bank, a number of meeting rooms, and a theater where a number of student productions are put on, as well as traveling shows from all over, and a bakery with some really good smoothies."

Q "The athletic complex is really, really nice, and computers are all hooked up to Ethernet, which is a really fast Internet connection. **The student center isn't really a big thing on campus**, but the bookstore is there as well as a food court."

Q "Everything is really nice; **the school is always remodeling or building new things** to keep the campus really looking elegant. The AC is quite nice, with a pool and exercise rooms that have plenty of treadmills and exercise machines to use. Almost all the computers are relatively new, so you shouldn't have a problem finding an adequate lab. Ditto for the student center."

The College Prowler Take On...
Facilities

The main facilities that students use on campus are the athletic complex (the AC), Mallinckrodt Center, the computer labs, and the libraries. Less demanding students find all of these satisfactory, but many agree that the athletic complex is a bit starved for resources. Equipment and space are lacking in many areas, although it's still possible to do a wide range of sports. Mallinckrodt serves as the provisional student center while a new one is under construction on the South 40. People can hang out in the Hilltop Café or bookstore upstairs, grab lunch at the food court downstairs, or get a tan in Bowles Plaza outside. As for libraries, they are all over campus, and they are mostly comfortable and well-stocked. The main library, Olin, for example, recently underwent a complete renovation.

Students in the sciences find the labs and buildings to be first-rate; in fact, the University recently built new lab sciences, earth and planetary sciences, and biomedical engineering buildings to keep up-to-date with new technologies and the BME boom. The arts have less lavish facilities, though this may change in the future. At the moment, for example, there is no performance facility for music students and amateur theater and opera groups; however, the massive new Sam Fox Arts Center will include a greatly enlarged museum of art, library, and exhibit space for student work. The actual physical look of Wash U's campus sharply divides people into die-hard supporters and detractors. The homogeneity of the Collegiate Gothic architecture is easy on the eyes to some, and deathly boring to others. A visit to campus will determine which perspective you take.

B-

The College Prowler® Grade on
Facilities: B-

A high Facilities grade indicates that the campus is aesthetically pleasing and well maintained, facilities are state-of-the-art, and libraries are exceptional. Other determining factors include the quality of both athletic and student centers, and an abundance of things to do on campus.

Campus Dining

The Lowdown On...
Campus Dining

Freshman Meal Plan Requirement?
Yes

Meal Plan Average Cost:
$3,754

Places to Grab a Bite with Your Meal Plan:

Arch/Art Cart
Location: Bixby
Food: Salads, bakery, soups
Favorite Dish: Cinnamon roll
Hours: Monday–Friday
8:30 a.m.–2:30 p.m.

Bear's Den
Location: Wohl Center
Food: American, bakery, salads

(Bear's Den, continued)

Favorite Dish: Filet mignon (seriously)

Hours: Monday–Thursday 7:30 a.m.– 2 a.m., Friday 7:30 a.m.–3 a.m., Saturday 11 a.m.–3 a.m., Sunday 11 p.m.–1 a.m.

Bear Mart

Location: Wohl Center

Food: Sandwiches, soups

Favorite Dish: Spicy Bowl Ramen Soup

Hours: Monday–Friday 10 a.m.–1 a.m., Saturday–Sunday 8:30 a.m.–1 a.m.

Café Olin

Location: Olin Hall

Food: Coffee, bakery

Favorite Dish: Bagel with flavored cream cheese

Hours: Monday–Thursday 8 a.m.–6:30 p.m.

Center Court

Location: Wohl Center

Food: Marketplace

Favorite Dish: Jerk chicken from the international counter

Hours: Monday–Thursday 6 p.m.–9 p.m., Saturday 11 a.m.–2 p.m., Sunday 11 a.m.–2 p.m., 6 p.m.–9 p.m.

Food Court

Location: Mallinckrodt

Food: Various

Favorite Dish: Spicy turkey and mashed potatoes

Hours: Monday–Friday 10:30 a.m.–3 p.m.

The Hilltop Bakery

Location: Mallinckrodt

Food: Bakery, smoothies

Favorite Dish: Krispy Kremes

Hours: Monday–Friday 7:30 a.m.–10 p.m., Saturday 8:30 a.m.– 5 p.m., Sunday 11 a.m.– 6 p.m.

Holmes Lounge

Location: Ridgley Hall

Food: Sandwiches, bakery

Favorite Dish: Yogurt

Hours: Monday–Friday 7:30 a.m.–3 p.m.

Law School Café

Location: Busch Hall

Food: Paninis, salads

Favorite Dish: Veggie panini

Hours: Monday–Thursday 8:15 a.m.–3:45 p.m., Friday 8:15 a.m.–2 p.m.

Lopata Cart

Location: Engineering Complex

Food: Hot dogs, sandwiches

Favorite Dish: Hot dog

Hours: Monday–Friday 10:30 a.m.–1:30 p.m.

Subway

Location: Old Rathskeller, behind Mallinckrodt

Food: Sandwiches

Favorite Dish: Pizza sub

Hours: Sunday–Thursday 10:30 a.m.–10 p.m., Friday–Saturday 10:30 a.m.–9 p.m.

Ursa's Café

Location: Under Lien Hall on the South 40

Food: Coffee, bakery, sushi

Favorite Dish: Blueberry scone

Hours: Monday–Sunday 6 p.m.–1 a.m.

The Village Café

Location: Small Group Housing

Food: Grill, International

Favorite Dish: Chicken quesadillas

Hours: Sunday–Thursday 8 a.m.–12 p.m., Friday–Saturday 5 p.m.–12 a.m.

24-Hour On-Campus Dining?

No

Student Favorites:

Holmes Lounge

The Village Café

Ursa's

Students Speak Out On...
Campus Dining

"For a college, I think dining at Wash U is not that bad, but I wouldn't say it's good either. I've been to other campuses, like Rice, and Wash U is definitely better, but it's nothing fantastic."

Q "Many students from other schools say that Wash U has some of the best food around. There are some all-you-can-eat options available for dinner and brunch on weekends. Everything else is á la carte. We also have **Subway and Taco Bell on campus, where you can use your meal plan**."

Q "On campus, **the food is actually pretty good**. We have the cafeteria and a deli-like place called Bear's Den on the South 40 (where most of the on-campus housing is located). On main campus, there are tons of places: Hilltop Bakery, Holmes Lounge, and Mallinckrodt which has a bunch of options like vegetarian, sushi, pasta, soul food, and more. Actually, our school's food was ranked second in the nation. I originally thought the food was good, but sometimes you do get sick of it. When that happens, there are plenty of cheap places nearby where you can get something to eat or good places that deliver."

Q "Our food's number two in the nation, but you'll probably **get sick of the food by the end of first year.** It's definitely high-quality and they have nice variations, but sometimes you'll still be frustrated. Center court is good for their vegan and vegetarian dishes. Bear's Den is open really late (1–2 a.m., depending on the day) and they have awesome chicken filets."

Q "To be honest, **food on campus is pretty bad**. Much of the food here tastes fine, but it's hard to eat healthy. However, over the years it has improved. I've heard that this past year it's gotten even better. There are two food courts on the South 40 called Center Court and Bear's Den. Bear's Den is open all day until about one in the morning, and it has things like spaghetti, sandwiches, fries, salad bar, yogurt, and a breakfast buffet. It is a social Mecca during afternoon hours."

Q "Center Court is a gigantic buffet-style place that is only open for dinner all week and offers brunch on the weekends. I thought it was pretty good. **There's always a big variety, and you can usually find what you want**. On the main campus (where you have your classes) there's one large building (called Mallinckrodt) that has sort of a food court like you'd find at the mall. The restaurants seem to change every few years, but last time I checked, there is a Subway, a Mexican place, a Chinese place, an Italian place, and a giant salad bar. Most students eat here for lunch during the day. There are a few other little places scattered around campus; one popular place, called Holmes, sells wraps and coffee."

Q "Dude, **the food here rocks**! I may be in the minority here, but I seriously think the food is really excellent at Wash U. Sometimes people complain about the lack of variety of food on campus, but I personally always feel like you can always find something to satisfy your taste buds. As far as good spots to grab a bite go: we've got Subway and Taco Bell if you're into fast food, Holmes lounge which is gorgeous and has tasty food, Center Court which offers an awesome unlimited buffet (they also have an incredible brunch there on Saturday and Sunday), and also available is the Small Group Housing Café which has things like shrimp, Moroccan food, and Indian food—I kid you not!"

Q "I've visited friends at other schools and the food here is actually quite good in comparison. **There's a lot of variety here**, so you don't get sick of eating the same thing every day. The main places to eat are Bear's Den and Center Court on the South 40. Bear's Den is kind of a sandwich and snack place (i.e., burgers, sandwich's, pasta, salad) while Center Court is more of, like, this huge buffet where, once you're in, it all-you-can-eat (everything you could think of). Center Court is really popular because your whole freshman floor goes together; it's really fun. Mallinckrodt has a huge food court with everything from Subway, Taco Bell, various pizzas, a salad bar with garden fresh veggies, Chinese, wraps, and so much more. This is a great place to grab a bite to eat between classes. There are also little cafés in some of the buildings, so you'll never lack for variety!"

Q "As far as good on-campus eating spots go, **Wash U does not disappoint**. Holmes Lounge is a student favorite. It opens up into the Quad, and on nice days it's an awesome place to hang out. They serve tons of wraps, paninis, and meats. Holmes Lounge is a beautiful place to study, too. It was the Queen's ballroom during the 1904 World's Fair. They now hold jazz concerts there in the summer. In the winter, they light up the fireplace and if you can grab a chair near it with a good cup of tea, you're set. Ursa's Cafe on the South 40 residential area is kind of fun. Students call it 'the Max,' like from *Saved by the Bell*. Ursa's has pool tables and table tops with board games built into them, so you can rent games like Sorry or Monopoly and play while you eat. It's got a big screen TV, a stage, computer kiosks, and an all-around friendly atmosphere. The food there is okay—it's generally the same as on campus: wraps, smoothies, soups, sushi, and salads."

The College Prowler Take On...
Campus Dining

College food is notorious for being bland, unhealthy, and expensive. Wash U is guilty on the last count, but the first two are at least up for debate. Wash U was, as many students mention, voted number two by "somebody" for the quality of the food service (it was actually *The Princeton Review*). How the ranking was determined is anyone's guess, but campus dining does offer a wide variety of possibilities, including a sushi bar and tasty vegetarian counter in the Mallinckrodt Center food court, custom-made omelettes and sirloin steak in the all-you-can-eat Centre Court, ethnic food and quesadillas in Small Group Housing, and fruit smoothies and custom ice cream at Ursa's. Although the majority here find the food to be quite good, most students eventually find campus food boring and monotonous—but students often say the same thing about their favorite off-campus restaurants, too.

In fact, it's possible to eat very well on campus, and although it isn't easy, it is possible to eat healthy as well (the frenetic pace of life at Wash U does make it hard to eat regular and balanced meals). Dining on campus is by no means cheap, though. Residents of the South 40 are required to purchase a meal plan, which can range from $3,474 to $3,816 per year (Kosher plans are more expensive). And even after students move off-campus, they are now required to purchase the Off-Campus Plan ($473). On-campus dining is convenient, but students who know how to cook for themselves will rightfully be in a hurry to get off campus, have their own kitchen, and save a couple thousand dollars by fixing their own meals.

B+

The College Prowler® Grade on Campus Dining: B+

Our grade on Campus Dining addresses the quality of both school-owned dining halls and independent on-campus restaurants, as well as the price, availability, and variety of food available.

Off-Campus Dining

The Lowdown On...
Off-Campus Dining

Restaurant Prowler: Popular Places to Eat!

Al-Tarboush Market and Deli
Food: Lebanese, Mediterranean
602 Westgate Ave., the Loop
(314) 725-1944
Cool features: Large selection of reasonably-priced hookahs
Price: $4–$6
Hours: Daily 11 a.m.–7:30 p.m.

Blueberry Hill
Food: Burgers
6504 Delmar Blvd., the Loop
(314) 727-0880
www.blueberryhill.com
Cool features: Rock and roll and '50s memorabilia, dart room, Chuck Berry plays monthly concerts, becomes a great bar at night
Price: $8–$10
Hours: Monday–Saturday 11 a.m.–1:30 a.m.,
Sunday 11 a.m.–12 a.m.

Brandt's Café
Food: International, grill
6525 Delmar Blvd.
(314) 727-3663
www.brandtscafe.com
Cool Features: Live music every night
Price: $8–$25
Hours: Monday–Thursday 11 a.m.–12 a.m., Friday–Saturday 11 a.m.–1 a.m., Sunday 10:30 a.m. –11:30 p.m.

Café Natasha
Food: Middle Eastern, vegetarian
3200 S. Grand Blvd.
(314) 771-3411
www.kabobinternational.com
Price: $4–$12
Hours: Sunday–Tuesday, Thursday 11:30 a.m.–9 p.m., Friday–Saturday 11:30 a.m.–10 p.m.

Crazy Bowls & Wraps
Food: International, vegetarian
7353 Forsyth Blvd.
University City
(314) 783-9727
www.crazybowlsandwraps.com
Price: $4–$5
Hours: Monday–Friday 10:30 a.m.–9 p.m., Saturday 11 a.m.–9 a.m., Sunday 11 a.m.–8 p.m.

Crazy Fish Bar and Grill
Food: American
15 North Meramec

(Crazy Fish, continued)
(314) 726-2111
Price: $15–$25
Hours: Monday–Thursday 11 a.m.–10 p.m., Friday–Saturday 11 a.m.–12 a.m., Sunday 11 a.m.–9 p.m.

Del Taco
Food: Taco Bell imitation
1033 McCausland
Phone: (314) 644-2615
www.deltaco.com
Cool Features: Dirt cheap
Price: $3–$7
Hours: 24-hour drive-thru

Duff's
Food: Pasta, steak, fish
392 N Euclid Ave.
(314) 361-0522
Price: $15–$17
Hours: Tuesday–Thursday 11 a.m.–10 p.m., Friday 11 a.m.–12 a.m., Saturday 10 a.m.–12 a.m., Sunday 10 a.m.–10 p.m.

Fitz's American Grill & Bottling Works
Food: American, bar, root beer
6605 Delmar Blvd., the Loop
(314) 726-9555
www.fitzsrootbeer.com
Price: $8–$15
Cool Features: Vintage root-beer bottler runs through the store

(Fitz's A, continued)
Hours: Monday–Thursday
11 a.m.–11 p.m., Friday–
Saturday 11 a.m.–12 a.m.,
Sunday 11 a.m.–10 p.m.

Hunan Star
Food: Chinese
1038 S Brentwood Blvd.
(314) 995-6982
Price: $6–$10
Hours: Sunday–Saturday
11 a.m.–9:30 p.m.

Int'l House of Pancakes (IHOP)
Food: Breakfast
8049 Clayton Rd.
(314) 725-8798
www.ihop.com
Cool features: Wash U special, all-you-can-eat pancakes for $3.59 after 5 p.m.
Price: $5–$8
Hours: Sunday–Thursday
5:30 a.m.–1 a.m., Friday–
Saturday 24 hours

Mama's Coal Pot
Food: St. Louis-style barbecue
6655 Delmar Blvd., the Loop
(314) 727-8034
Price: $3–$6
Hours: Monday–Saturday
11 a.m.–3 p.m.

MP O'Reillys
Food: Wings, drinks
5627 Manchester Ave.

(MP O'Reillys, continued)
(314) 781-4487
www.mporeillys.com
Price: $8–$20
Hours: Monday–Friday
4 p.m.–3 a.m.,
Saturday 8 p.m.– 3 a.m.,
Sunday 9 a.m.–3 a.m.

Portabella
Food: Italian
15 N Central Ave., Clayton
(314) 725-6593
Price: $10–$30
Hours: Monday–Thursday
11 a.m.–2 p.m.,
5:30 p.m.–10 p.m., Friday–
Saturday 11 a.m.–10:30 p.m.,
Sunday 5 p.m.–9 p.m.

Racanelli's
Food: Italian, pizza
6655 Delmar Blvd., the Loop
(314) 727-7227
www.creativeon-line.com/racanellisloop.html
Price: $5–$20
Hours: Sunday–Thursday
11 a.m.–9 p.m., Friday–
Saturday 11 a.m.–10 p.m.

Thai Café
Food: Thai
6170 Delmar Blvd., the Loop
(314) 862-6868
Price: $8–$12
Hours: Monday–Friday
11:30 a.m.–10 p.m.,
Saturday 5 p.m.–10 p.m.

Thai Country Café
Food: Thai
6223 Delmar Blvd., the Loop
(314) 862-0787
Cool Features: Cheap food, bizarre Thai/American West restaurant theme.
Price: $3–$9
Hours: Monday, Wednesday–Friday 11:30 a.m.–3 p.m., 5 p.m.–10 p.m., Saturday–Sunday 11:30 a.m.–10 p.m.

TJ's Wild Flower Restaurant
Food: International, pizza
4590 Laclede Ave., South End
(314) 367-9888
Price: $10–$15
Hours: Sunday–Monday 11 a.m.–10 p.m., Wednesday–Thursday 11 a.m.–10 p.m., Friday–Saturday 11 a.m.–11 p.m.

Wong's Wok
Food: Cheap Chinese
6655 Delmar Blvd., the Loop
(314) 726-0976
Price: $2–$6
Hours: Monday–Saturday 11 a.m.–9 p.m.

Zoë Pan-Asia Café
Food: Innovative, neo-Asian
4753 McPherson at Euclid Ave.
(314) 361-0013
Price: $13–$15
Hours: Monday–Thursday 11:30 a.m.–2:30 p.m., 5:30 p.m.–10 p.m.
Friday 11:30 a.m.–2:30 p.m., 5:30 p.m.–11 p.m.,
Saturday 5 p.m.–11 p.m.,
Sunday 5 p.m.–10 p.m.

Did You Know?

The **Anheuser-Busch brewing company** (maker of Budweiser, Busch, and Bud Light), which is based in St. Louis, offers daily tours of its historic brewery, complete with beer tasting, for visitors 21-and-over. Anheuser-Busch is also a proud sponsor of Wash U, and the main law school building is named Anheuser-Busch Hall. Let's just hope that these future attorneys don't drink on the job.

Other Places to Check Out:
Addi's
Applebee's
Cicero's
Cunetto's Gyro House
Harvest
India's Rasoi
The Jade Room
Killkenny's Pub
Melting Pot
Outback Steakhouse
Pho Grand
Riddle's Penultimate Café & Wine Bar
Rossino's
St. Louis Bread Co.
Tomatillo Mexican Grill
Yemanja Brasil

Student Favorites:
Al-Tarboush
Crazy Bowls & Wraps
Mama's Coal Pot
Wong's Wok

Grocery Stores:
Schnucks
6600 Clayton Rd.
(314) 644-0510

Whole Foods (organic)
1601 S. Brentwood Blvd.
(314) 968-7744

Wild Oats (organic)
8823 Ladue Rd.
(314) 721-8004

24-Hour Eating:
Del Taco, IHOP

Best Breakfast:
IHOP

Best Chinese:
Hunan Star, Wong's Wok

Best Healthy:
Al-Tarboush Market
Café Natasha
Whole Foods

Best Pizza:
Racanelli's

Best Wings:
MP O'Reillys

Best Place to Take Your Parents:
Crazy Fish
Duff's
Zoë Pan-Asian Café

Students Speak Out On...
Off-Campus Dining

> "St. Louis has great places to dine. Without cars, freshmen are limited, but the Loop is within walking distance of campus and has tons of fun, funky restaurants and shops. It's also a great place for Wash U students to meet students from other schools."

"One place to visit near campus is what we call 'cheap Chinese,' also known as Wong's Wok. It's a little stand at the far end of the market in the Loop building. They have wonderful dirt cheap fried rice and combo plates. **An absolute must in the Loop is Cunetto's Gyro House**. The jumbo gyro there, with the special hot sauce (you have to ask for it) is just amazing!"

"There are some pretty good restaurants near Wash U. **The Loop is a pretty cool area** like ten minutes walking distance from campus. There is a place called Fitz's which is famous for its root beer. There is Thai food at the Thai Country Café, Mexican at Tomatillo's, and all other kinds of good stuff."

"The Melting Pot is a very popular fondue restaurant in St. Louis. The thing is, **without a car you will probably not find yourself going off campus to eat** that much your first year. There is this place called the Loop that has a lot of nice shops and restaurants, and it is within walking distance; but again, going off campus to eat was just a nice treat every once in a while. I like the food here enough to stay on campus and settle for cafeteria food."

Q "**There are a bunch of good restaurants** near Wash U. There are traditional chains like Outback Steakhouse and Applebee's, and lesser-known eateries for daring eaters that serve Turkish food and Thai. There is a mall nearby, as well. The campus has shuttles that run every 15 minutes to the mall and supermarkets, as well as the surrounding apartment areas. The shuttle also makes stops at public transportation centers, including several Metrolink train stations. It is very easy to get around the city with no car, and even easier with one."

Q "My favorite off-campus restaurants are: **Café Natasha**, which is quite pricey; Thai Country Café, which is definitely affordable; and Harvest, which is very expensive. Harvest is totally a place your parents can take you when they come to visit. There are tons of other restaurants around campus that are also worth eating at."

Q "St Louis has **lots of ethnic restaurants**. In Clayton (right near Wash U), there are many restaurants with good food that students can afford. St. Louis also has a lot of Italian restaurants in the Hill, the Italian section of the city."

Q "There's almost every type of food in St. Louis, with the exception of many good sushi or Chinese food places. However, there's really good Italian, Thai, and eclectic American restaurants **all within walking- or driving-distance**. Some of the best places I've found are Crazy Bowls & Wraps, St. Louis Bread Co. (those two are reasonably priced), Brandt's, Crazyfish, Wild Flower, Zoë, Thai Country Cafe, Cunetto's, and Portabella."

Q "Wash U is right by the University City Loop, which is a small shopping district on a street called Delmar. It's a street known for its history. There are no clubs or anything like that, but **there are many good restaurants and boutiques**. Blueberry Hill is one of the best bar-and-grilles in the country, and Wash U students have it at their fingertips. They bring in great live music, and have for decades; it's a great place to go on Thursday nights for a beer and giant burger. You'll always run into someone you know there. Fitz's, Thai Country Cafe, Cicero's, Brandt's, and Riddle's are also all on Delmar. These are great places to go grab a quick bite and sit on the patio. There are lots of Wash U kids everywhere."

Q "The **Central West End is a good place to go for food**. You have really upscale dining, like Zoë Pan-Asian and Cafe Balaban. The Wild Flower (awesome place to get a bottle of wine, sit on the patio, and draw all over the tables with crayons), Rossino's, and Dëuffs all serve finger foods at cheap prices (under $10 for any entrée). The Grand area, closer to Saint Louis University, also has some cool places to go and eat. The Jade Room and Pho Grand are located there, and they are great places to take a date. And the Clayton area just west of Wash U has some good restaurants and bars, too, like Killkenny's Pub and Portabella. Then, the Hill is famous for Italian food eateries, and the Soulard area has made St. Louis Mardi Gras the second largest celebration in the country."

The College Prowler Take On...
Off-Campus Dining

It's always nice to venture off campus to find a more exotic, romantic, or classy atmosphere for dining. Fortunately, St. Louis offers a wide variety of cuisine, from Thai and Vietnamese, to Jamaican, Brazilian, and German. A number of fine restaurants lie within walking distance of the campus, especially in Clayton (Portabella, Crazy Fish, Miso, and Il Vicino are some student favorites); the University City Loop is popular, as well. More exotic cuisine usually requires a car trip, however. For example, the fabulous India's Rasoi, which is located in the Central West End, or Yemanja Brasil, nestled deep in mid-town St. Louis on Pestalozzi, are both must-eats, but are not within walking-distance.

Affordable, quick meals are certainly available in the nearby Loop area. Everyone who discovers the Middle Eastern flavors of Cunetto's Gyro House and Al Tarboush becomes a regular customer. And Brandt's and Addi's offer more refined dining, for a date or for dinner with visiting relatives, all just a few blocks from campus. In all, with some looking, diners will find that almost every range of price, flavor, and atmosphere imaginable exists among St. Louis restaurants.

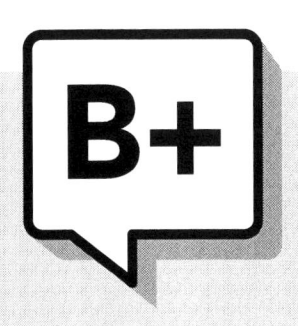

B+

The College Prowler® Grade on Off-Campus Dining: B+

A high Off-Campus Dining grade implies that off-campus restaurants are affordable, accessible, and worth visiting. Other factors include the variety of cuisine and the availability of alternative options (vegetarian, vegan, Kosher, etc.).

Campus Housing

The Lowdown On...
Campus Housing

Undergrads Living on Campus:
73%

Number of Dormitories:
25

Best Dorms:
Danforth
Hitzeman
Hurd
Koenig
Liggett
Myers

Worst Dorms:
Gregg
Lien
Nemerov

Dormitories:

Wash U dorms are arranged in residential colleges—a grouping of two or more halls which combine as one community to promote personal growth for students. However, as you'll see, each individual hall is very different from the next.

Beaumont Hall

Floors: 3, plus basement
Total Occupancy: 150
Bathrooms: Shared with floor
Coed: Yes, single-sex by floor
Residents: All freshmen
Room Types: Double, single, triple
Special Features: Laundry room, study room, TV lounge, computer cluster, substance-free building

Danforth Hall

Floors: 4, plus basement
Total Occupancy: 196
Bathrooms: Shared by suite
Coed: Yes, single-sex by suite
Residents: All freshmen
Room types: Suite, double, triple, forced-triple
Special Features: Laundry room, TV lounge, study lounges, library, multipurpose room, computer cluster

Dauten Hall

Floors: 4, plus basement
Total Occupancy: 90

(Dauten Hall, continued)

Bathrooms: Shared by suite
Coed: Yes, single-sex by suite
Residents: Mostly sophomores
Room Types: 15 six-person suites with two singles and two doubles
Special Features: Laundry room, computer cluster, study lounge, piano practice rooms, balconies

Eliot Hall

Floors: 4
Total Occupancy: 156
Bathrooms: Shared between suites, triples have private
Coed: Yes, by suite
Residents: Upperclassmen
Room Types: Single, double, triple—all suites
Special Features: Laundry room, computer cluster, study/TV lounges, living rooms, multipurpose room, kitchenette

Forsyth House

Floors: 4, plus health center
Total Occupancy: 169
Bathrooms: Shared by suite, some private
Coed: Yes, single-sex by suite
Residents: All freshmen
Room Types: doubles suite, double, triple
Special Features: Substance-free floor, study lounges, computer cluster, common room, laundry room, library, some classrooms

Gregg Hall
Floors: 8, plus basement
Total Occupancy: 160
Bathrooms: Shared by suite, some private
Coed: Yes, single-sex by suite
Residents: All upperclassmen
Room Types: Three or four single rooms to a suite, doubles
Special Features: Laundry room, computer lab, study lounge, TV lounge

Hitzeman Hall
Floors: 4, plus basement
Total Occupancy: 90
Bathrooms: In room
Coed: Yes, single-sex by suite
Residents: All upperclassmen
Room Types: 15 six-person suites with two singles and two doubles
Special Features: Laundry room, computer cluster, study room, balconies, dance studio

Hurd Hall
Floors: 4, plus basement
Total Occupancy: 74
Bathrooms: Shared by suite
Coed: Yes, single-sex by suite
Residents: No freshmen
Room Types: 14 six-person suites with two singles and two doubles; two eight-person suites, all doubles
Special Features: Laundry room, computer cluster, study lounge, piano practice rooms, balconies

Koenig Hall
Floors: 3, plus basement
Total Occupancy: 150
Bathrooms: Shared by floor
Coed: Yes, single-sex by suite
Residents: All freshmen
Room Types: Singles, doubles, and triples, all suites
Special Features: TV lounge, study lounge, laundry room, computer cluster

Lee Hall
Floors: 3, plus basement
Total Occupancy: 150
Bathrooms: Shared by floor
Coed: Yes, single-sex by the wing or by the suite
Residents: All freshmen
Room Types: Singles, doubles, and triples, and suites
Special Features: Laundry room, common spaces, kitchen, multipurpose room, study room, computer cluster

Lien
Floors: 4, plus faculty offices
Total Occupancy: 163
Bathrooms: Shared by floor
Coed: Yes, single-sex by suite
Residents: All freshman
Room Types: Doubles, triples, all suites
Special Features: Laundry room, multipurpose room, computer cluster, library, study room, living room

Liggett Hall

Floors: 3, plus basement
Total Occupancy: 150
Bathrooms: Shared by floor
Coed: Yes, single-sex by suite
Residents: All freshmen
Room Types: Four single rooms to a suite or two double rooms to a suite
Special Features: TV lounge, study lounge, laundry room, computer cluster

Lopata

Floors: 3, plus basement
Total Occupancy: 155
Bathroom: Two half baths to four single rooms
Coed: Yes, by the suite
Residents: Upperclassmen
Room Types: Four larger single rooms to a suite
Special Features: Basement classrooms, computer cluster, formal room called "the Great Room," large multipurpose room, one large kitchen, three kitchenettes and lounges on each floor

Mudd Hall

Floors: 3, plus basement
Total Occupancy: 80
Bathroom: Shared by suite
Coed: Yes, single-sex by suite
Residents: Mostly seniors
Room Types: Four large single rooms to one suite, two large double rooms to one suite

(Mudd Hall, continued)

Special Features: Only building with living room with large windows, computer cluster, TV lounge, study lounge, laundry rooms and kitchens on every floor

Myers Hall

Floors: 4, plus basement
Total Occupancy: 90
Bathrooms: Shared by suite
Coed: Yes, single-sex by suite
Residents: All upperclassmen
Room Types: 14 six-person suites with two singles and two doubles; two eight-person suites, both doubles
Special Features: Laundry room, computer cluster, balconies, music practice rooms

Nemerov Hall

Floors: 4 floors
Total Occupancy: 137
Bathroom: Shared by suite
Coed: Yes, single-sex by suite
Residents: All upperclassmen
Room Types: Suites, doubles
Special Features: Recreation area, TV lounge, study lounges, laundry room, computer cluster, project rooms

Park Hall

Floors: 3, plus basement
Total Occupancy: 80
Bathroom: Shared by suite
Coed: Yes, single-sex by suite

(Park Hall, continued)

Residents: All upperclassmen

Room Types: Four single person rooms to a suite; two double person rooms to a suite

Special Features: Recreation area, TV lounge, study lounge, laundry room, computer cluster

Rubelmann Hall

Floors: 3, plus basement

Total Occupancy: 150

Bathrooms: Shared by floor

Coed: Yes, single-sex by room

Residents: All freshmen

Room Types: Traditional singles, doubles, and triples

Special Features: TV lounge, study lounges, laundry room, ping-pong tables

Rutledge Hall

Floors: 4, plus basement

Total Occupancy: 90

Bathrooms: Shared by suite

Coed: Yes, single-sex by suite

Residents: All upperclassmen

Room Types: Six- and eight-person suites

Special Features: Laundry room, computer cluster, study lounge, piano practice rooms, photography studio

Shanedling Hall

Floors: 4 plus basement

Total Occupancy: 90

Bathrooms: Shared by suite

Coed: Yes, single-sex by suite

Residents: All upperclassmen

Room Types: Six- and eight-person suites

Special Features: Laundry room, computer cluster, study lounge, piano practice rooms

Shepley Hall

Floors: 4 plus basement

Total Occupancy: 120

Bathrooms: Shared by the suite, some private

Coed: Yes, single-sex by suite

Residents: No freshmen

Room Types: Four-person suites, single or double rooms

Special Features: Laundry room, project rooms, computer cluster, TV lounge, study lounges

Small Houses 9 and 10

Floors: Two connected row houses of four floors

Total Occupancy: 48

Bathrooms: Shared by floor

Coed: Yes, single-sex by floor

Residents: All upperclassmen

Room Types: Singles

Special Features: Laundry room, computer cluster, common areas, TV lounge

Umrath Hall

Floors: 3 plus basement

Total Occupancy: 150

Bathrooms: Shared by Floor

Coed: Yes, single-sex by room

Residents: All freshmen

(Umrath Hall, continued)

Room Types: Traditional singles, doubles, and triples

Special Features: TV lounge, study lounge, laundry room, ping-pong tables

Village House

Floors: 4; no housing on bottom floor

Total Occupancy: 147

Bathrooms: Shared by a suite

Coed: Yes, single-sex by suites

Residents: All upperclassmen

Room Types: Large single suites

Special Features: Common area with fireplace, four dining rooms, basement classrooms, lounges and kitchenettes on each floor

Wheeler Hall

Floors: 4, plus basement

Total Occupancy: 151

Bathrooms: Shared by suite, some private

Coed: Yes

Residents: All upperclassmen

Room Types: Four single-person rooms make up a suite; two doubles make up a suite

Special Features: Laundry room, project rooms, TV lounge, study lounges, computer cluster

Room Types

Residence Halls include single, double, triple (sometimes forced triples), and suite-style units.

Single – students have their own room and share a common bathroom with their floormates.

Double, Triple – student shares a room with one or two other students, and a common bathroom with the floor.

Suite-style – students share a semi-private bathroom and a common living area.

Bed Type

Extra-long twin (33"x 80"); some lofts, some bunk-beds

Available for Rent

Mini-fridge

Cleaning Service?

Yes. Professional cleaning is available in public areas. Community and semi-private bathrooms are cleaned by staff approximately once-a-week.

You Get

Bed, desk, chair, bookshelf, dresser, closet or wardrobe, window coverings, telephone, cable TV jack, Ethernet or broadband Internet connections

Also Available

Substance-free living option, special-interest housing (in Small Group Housing)

Did You Know?

Every year, the South 40 hosts the Residential College Olympics, a fierce sporting extravaganza in which dorms square off in football, soccer, ping-pong, ultimate Frisbee, chess, a 5K run, pool, and other sporting events for the honor of being named "Best Residential College."

Old vs. New

Wash U's main residential campus, the South 40, is divided between traditional housing complexes with shared bathrooms and few amenitiesas known as the "old dorms", as well as several recently constructed, more luxurious facilities known as the "new dorms." There is a popular rivalry on campus as to which dorms are superior.

Old Dorms:

Beaumont
Dauten
Hitzeman
Hurd
Lee
Liggett
Myers
Rubelmann
Rutledge
Shanedling
Umrath

New Dorms:

Danforth
Eliot
Forsyth
Gregg
Koenig
Lien
Nemerov
Shepley
Wheeler

Students Speak Out On...
Campus Housing

> "The dorms are all pretty nice, and the rooms are big compared to other schools. Personally, I lived in the old dorms and I loved it. The new dorms are really nice, too, but a different atmosphere. They're all great."

Q "I'm definitely an advocate of the old dorms. In the new dorms, everyone's in their own suites with their own bathrooms. I feel like there are a lot more closed doors, and **lots less opportunities for interaction**. In the old dorms, you can just look down the hall and see which rooms are open, which is pretty sweet, and the common bathrooms make for a more social atmosphere. It was also fun to be able to look down the hall and see a girl in a towel, walking to take a shower."

Q "**Where you choose to live your freshman year is very important**. I chose the substance-free dorm, and it was the best decision I ever made. If you like to party, you still get the chance at the frats and things like that. If you decide to live in a non-substance-free dorm, you'll find yourself surrounded by people who are on their own for the first time and it will turn into a 24-hour party, which is fine until you want to sleep or work (or until you get your grades). In the old dorms, there's also usually a lot of trash and puke that you have to deal with on the way to your room on party nights. You really don't have that problem in substance-free dorms."

Q "The dorms are nice. Lien and Danforth are the new freshmen dorms. **Stay away from Beaumont, though**. The RAs (resident assistants) there are too strict."

Q "I loved dorm life. **Avoid living in a triple**, if you can, as it gets kind of cramped. I would recommend living in one of the older buildings your freshman year, even though the newer ones seem nicer. The newer buildings look pretty, but they are not in any way soundproofed, and the walls fall off when you take down a poster. Plus, the layout of the older buildings is such that it's easier to talk to people and meet people who live on your floor. I'd avoid the suites (two people sharing a bathroom) for this reason, as well: if everything you need in the dorm is within your room (i.e., bathroom), you have less reason to wander through the halls and you end up becoming more of a hermit. If you're shy, you have to make more of an effort to meet people. Of course, if you're super outgoing, you'll find your particular scene, regardless. Overall, though, all of the dorms are nice. There aren't any I would panic over."

Q "Some of the dorms are **really nice, like Lien and Danforth**, but they aren't very social. I lived in Koenig and really loved it."

Q "As a freshman, you have a choice between the old dorms and the new dorms. I was in the new dorms. Basically, **the old dorms are much more social and fun**, but one negative is that there are communal bathrooms. In the new dorms, it feels like you're in a Comfort Inn, but it's not as social. However, you share a bathroom and shower with only one other double, so that's nice."

Q "The dorms are **actually pretty decent here**. I lived in Rubelmann Hall. Rubelmann is in a very good location because it's close to the cafeterias and classroom buildings."

Q "**Dorms at Wash U are awesome**! I've been so pleased thus far. I'd say, as a freshman, go for the old dorms. They've got more character, and they're way more social. I'd say the best dorms to live in as a freshman are Liggett, Koenig, Rubelmann, Umrath, or Lee. Those are all coed dorms (though if you're interested in living in a same-sex floor, there is one available for females) and they're comprised of mostly doubles, with a few singles and triples. They've also got communal bathrooms. Seriously, the old dorms are not bad or gross at all, and you will, I promise you, meet and chill with your best friends in the bathroom."

Q "If you'd rather not deal with a communal bathroom, then choose the new dorms. Danforth and Lien offer suite-style living, meaning that there's four people to a bathroom. **The new dorms also have larger rooms** and are nicer because they are newer. However, new dorms are more expensive and do tend to attract the nerdiest of nerds. They're still cool, though, and my friends who lived there definitely enjoyed themselves. Choose Danforth over Lien, though."

Q "**One dorm to avoid is definitely Beaumont**. That's the substance-free dorm where many of the students are ridiculously weird and anti-social. Drink or don't drink, it's cool either way, but trust me on the non-substance-free thing—your social life will thank me for it!"

Q "All the dorms are nice; again, it's your choice to live in an old or new dorm. The new dorms are obviously the nicest, but **the old dorms still have their charm**. I actually lived in one of the old dorms my freshman year and loved it because everyone was so social and we all really bonded. As for new dorms, should you so choose, I'd say Lien."

Q "The new dorms are nice because they look like ski lodges, with Lien House and Danforth being the nicest. The other freshmen dorms are old, but more social. In the new dorms, everyone gets a four-person suite and you share a bathroom, but everyone seems to stay to themselves. The doors for each room shut automatically so you can't just leave them open and let your neighbors pop in and out. The old dorms are much more open and people can wander in and out of your room if you leave the doors open. Plus, there are community bathrooms. It depends on your tastes, but I think you meet more people in the old dorms. **Most people move off campus after their sophomore year**, but you can stay on if you like. The sophomore suites are old, but they have balconies. There are six people to a suite, two singles, two doubles, one bathroom, and one common room in sophomore suites. The new sophomore suites are like the freshman dorms. They're really nice, but not as open."

The College Prowler Take On...
Campus Housing

Each of the dorms clustered on the cozy residential campus known as the South 40 has its own distinctive flavor and atmosphere. These particularities often produce fierce loyalties and rivalries between the students who live there—especially between the residents of the old dorms and new dorms. Proponents of the old dorms hold that the social interaction, sense of floor unity, and genuine gritty college experience they find in their halls cannot be matched by the posh, but sterile new towers nearby. The new dorms have what seem like material benefits, like semi-private bathrooms, elevators, and floor kitchens, but sharing a common bathroom in the old dorms means two kids can strike up a conversation while brushing their teeth. The narrow halls and low lighting of the old dorms give a conspiratorial aura to floor life, a sort of "we're all in this together" vibe that contrasts starkly with the "we're all just paying rent here" vibe of the new dorms.

For first-year students in particular, the old dorms (especially Liggett, Umrath, and Rubelmann) foster a terrific atmosphere for meeting people and becoming acclimated to a new environment. The only downside to the old dorms is the lack of amenities. It's next to impossible to do any kind of cooking in the old buildings, and none of the old freshman dorms have piano practice rooms or pleasant study lounges as the new dorms do. After freshman year, the old dorms still remain a good option, though. The sophomore suites (Hurd, Hitzeman, Myers, Rutledge, Shanedling, and Dauten), which are equipped with balconies, furniture, and a huge common room, must have been designed with college parties in mind.

B+

The College Prowler® Grade on
Campus Housing: B+

A high Campus Housing grade indicates that dorms are clean, well-maintained, and spacious. Other determining factors include variety of dorms, proximity to classes, and social atmosphere.

Off-Campus Housing

The Lowdown On...
Off-Campus Housing

Undergrads in Off-Campus Housing:
27%

Average Rent For:
1BR Apt:. $500/month
2BR Apt.: $850/month

Best Time to Look for a Place:
Beginning of second semester

Popular Places:
Washington Ave.
Kingsbury Ave.
Kingsland Ave.

For Assistance Contact:
Quadrangle Housing Company
700 Rosedale Ct.
www.offcampushousing.wustl.edu
Phone: (314) 935-9511
E-Mail: ars@restech.wustl.edu
Hours: Monday–Friday
8:30 a.m.–5 p.m.

Did You Know?

The University uses a **lottery system** to assign housing. Fraternity members are automatically assigned terrible lottery numbers.

Students Speak Out On...
Off-Campus Housing

"Next year, I'm living off campus, but I'm glad I lived on campus for a few years. It was an amazing experience, but now I'm ready to have my own place. I found the location on my own, but the school does provide lots of off-campus apartments and houses that are really nice."

Q "Living off campus is just as convenient as living on campus. Being closer to **the Loop is great, and you're just as close to campus**. Off-campus living also gives you a feel of what life will be like after graduation. There are some bad apartments out there, but if you get an apartment in University City or within a few blocks of Skinker in St. Louis, you'll be in a good spot."

Q "**Housing off campus is very convenient**. Wash U owns apartments on campus and off campus. These usually fill up quickly and there's a lottery to get them. However, there are a million non-Wash U-owned apartments in the same area, and they're usually pretty affordable. Most people move off campus their sophomore year or move into the suites on campus (which are like apartments without kitchens). Most students who live off campus live just north of the school or northeast of the school in a pretty neighborhood that's bursting with trees. Most of the apartments seem to house students, but there are also other residents of the city who live there, as well. Opportunities are abundant."

Q "I was able to find several babysitting jobs in walking-distance. The Loop is on the other side of the neighborhood. Everything about the area is nice, except that the surrounding area (the other side of the Loop) isn't so great. Therefore, **it's dangerous to be out by yourself at night**. However, if you live in this area, you still are able to use a lot of the campus services such as the shuttle, and there are blue-light emergency phones prevalent."

Q "One of the really great things about Wash U is that, if you choose to live off campus, **Wash U owns a ton of apartments within walking-distance**, so it's really nice. You can technically live off campus but still have Wash U conveniences like telephone and Internet lines. There are also a set of apartment buildings right on the corner of campus that still offer the apartment experience (e.g., kitchen, living room, etc.)"

Q "**My two friends and I quickly got an apartment through the Wash U off-campus lottery**, but not everybody had it so easy. We all had good lottery numbers, so we got our first choice on a sweet apartment on Kingsbury. Parkview Properties is the service we went through, although I've heard that some private realtors are good, too, like Roberts Realty. I know some students who didn't get anything in any of the lotteries, and by that time, almost all of the privately-owned apartments were filled and they got stuck with a crappy place."

Q "I totally recommend staying away from Waterman! I lived down there junior year. It's not that far from campus and it's cheap, but it's far from the Loop, and in terms of parties and seeing people, **University City is such a better option**. Rosedale, in particular, which is a Wash U housing option on Waterman (east of Skinker), is completely dead. Don't go there!"

"I was a transfer student my sophomore year. I got placed off-campus with two girls I didn't know because I transferred too late to plan my own housing, and I really wish they hadn't done that! **I wish I could have started out on campus**, met lots of people, and gone to parties and all that. My roommates were completely boring! I pledged a sorority, though, and now I'm living off campus with one of my sisters."

The College Prowler Take On...
Off-Campus Housing

By junior year, moving off of the South 40 becomes a very attractive option for most students. Most upperclassmen decide to find an apartment in a nearby residential area, either through the University's Parkview Properties subcontractor, the Apartment Referral Service, or through a private realtor. University City seems the most popular area, since it has a few blocks almost entirely populated by Wash U students. There are centrally located apartments east of Skinker and north of Delmar, as well, which are less popular but have generally cheaper rent. The Wash U-owned apartments tend to be more expensive than privately-owned ones, but they have the benefit of amenities like Ethernet, laundry rooms, and package utilities.

There is fierce competition for the choice apartments, of course. Many are now owned by Wash U, so your lottery number and those of your roommates will be decisive in whether or not you get something through the Wash U housing process. For the private route, the key is to first find someone living in an apartment you like who will be leaving next year (either by word of mouth or by knocking on doors). Get them to sign a sheet saying they'll turn over the lease to you at the end of their contract, and you're set. Many apartments are handed down from friend to friend this way, but there's always the old-fashioned door-to-door option, which has been known to work on occasion.

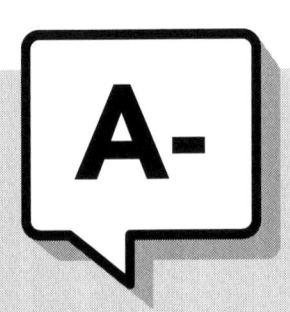

A-

The College Prowler® Grade on
Off-Campus Housing: A-

A high grade in Off-Campus Housing indicates that apartments are of high quality, close to campus, affordable, and easy to secure.

Diversity

The Lowdown On...
Diversity

African American:
10%

Asian American:
14%

Hispanic:
4%

International:
5%

Native American:
Less than 1%

White:
59%

Unknown:
8%

Out-of-State:
90%

Political Activity

The campus is pretty well divided up into two small fringes, conservative and liberal, and a big neutral mass in the middle. Though the campus has its share of protests, students are generally not outspoken about their political views. Many consider the student body to be generally apathetic about politics.

Gay Pride

The gay community isn't particularly outspoken on campus, but it has a large GLBT club called Spectrum Alliance which organizes an awareness week and other events.

Most Popular Religions

There are a lot of Jewish students on campus, but Christian groups are more numerous and active.

Economic Status

A large majority of Wash U students are quite wealthy.

Sampling of Minority Clubs

Wash U has a number of Asian American, African American, Hispanic, and Indian American clubs that throw parties and sponsor different events. There are also seven African American Greek organizations, an Asian fraternity, two Jewish fraternities, and one Jewish sorority.

Students Speak Out On...
Diversity

"Wash U is not that diverse. There are a few minority students here, but there isn't that much interaction between them. Black students tend to live in Park and Mudd Halls, Asians live off campus with each other, and nobody mixes much. I wish it were more diverse."

Q "I would say our campus is pretty diverse compared to other schools. Definitely more so than other private schools I looked at. There are a lot of Asian and Hispanic students on campus. I would say those two groups are the biggest of the minority groups. **Our school also has a very large Jewish student population**. A lot of the students here are Jewish. I think we have a good mix of students attending Wash U."

Q "I come from a very diverse community (Ann Arbor, MI), so I've found it hard to find areas that compare, but Wash U is about as close as you can get. **You certainly don't feel like you're surrounded by only white people**. There is a large Indian population, Asian population, and African American population. I certainly didn't feel like I was starving for culture. There are a number of very popular student-organizations for different ethnic communities; the Indian student organization puts on a show every year, the Japanese student group has a festival, the Hawaii club (which I was a part of) puts on a luau, and there are other events as well."

Q "From what I just read the other day in the newspaper, there are **lots of Jewish people and Asians** that attend Wash U. However, a lot of times, the different groups tend to keep together. I personally didn't see minorities around here too much."

Q "Wash U is **not as diverse as I'd like it to be**, but we're pretty good compared to other places. Something that bugs me is that, even though we're diverse on paper, a lot of times people who are of the same race tend to stick together and not really hang out with people of a different culture than them. That's kind of lame."

Q "In many ways, Wash U is a relatively **homogenous place**, in that most students tend to be well-off, American (the international community is small), and pretty conventional in their political and cultural views (i.e., somewhat conservative or unengaged). That said, minority groups contribute a lot to campus diversity with events like the Chinese New Year Festival, or Diwali the break-dancing club, or the Korean barbecues. But diversity is, in fact, one of Wash U's problem areas. There are people from all over the country, and sometimes the world, but they often resemble each other socioeconomically and politically and reinforce the homogeneity of the campus."

The College Prowler Take On...
Diversity

Along the main walkway between Graham Chapel and Brookings Hall, banners recruiting members for Jewish, Christian, Muslim, black, Korean, Indian, and gay groups flutter overhead, at least giving the impression that Wash U enjoys a diverse and open-minded community. While three quarters of the student body is white, Wash U does enjoy the presence of active and outspoken minority groups. As on many campuses, though, minorities often stick together and have their own clubs, parties, and dorms. Among the more social slice of Wash U undergrads, though, there are no ethnic lines. Blacks, whites, Indian-Americans, Korean-Americans, Jews, and Catholics all party together, become fraternity brothers and sorority sisters, and share community service activities. The cultural interests of the average Wash U kid (beer-pong, TV sports, and video games) unite a big part of the population across different family backgrounds and the whole spectrum of skin colors.

In terms of life experiences, Wash U's undergrads are not as diverse. Generally wealthy, they have led charmed lives and aren't typically the adventurous, risk-taking sort. Not many Wash U students come from disadvantaged financial situations, working class families, or have international backgrounds. Further, a large proportion of Wash U students have, for one reason or another, similar career interests. Pre-medicine, engineering, and business dominate (making up over 40 percent of all undergrads), giving a less liberal-artsy and more corporate feel to the student body.

B-

The College Prowler® Grade on

Diversity: B-

A high grade in Diversity indicates that ethnic minorities and international students have a notable presence on campus, and that students of different economic backgrounds, religious beliefs, and sexual preferences are well-represented.

Guys & Girls

The Lowdown On...
Guys & Girls

Female Undergrads:
50%

Male Undergrads:
40%

Birth Control Available?

Yes. Female students who have had an exam with their home doctor or have an exam with Health Services can have their birth control prescriptions filled at health services for $10. Health Services offers all forms of birth control, including pills, patches, and the shot. They also provide free condoms.

Social Scene

The Wash U social scene has a fairly dominant fraternity/sorority set, which acts as the center for a lot of the on-campus and off-campus parties. While Greek membership on campus is roughly 25 percent, a majority those students who go out regularly choose to join a frat or sorority. Of course, the obligatory sub-cultures have their place at Wash U, as well: the stoners, the KWUR (Wash U radio) crowd, the jocks, the artsy crowd; but many members of those sub-cultures are Greek members as well!

Hookups or Relationships?

Hookups are quite common during freshman and sophomore years, although by junior and senior year, people tend to get more serious and look for long-term relationships. Wash U kids, like any other group of college students, have their needs, though, so it's not uncommon for random hookups to occur all the way through senior year.

Dress Code

Wash U kids don't get too creative with their appearance, and they stick with the clean-cut, classy look. Polos, button-downs, or T-shirts, with khakis or jeans are standard for guys; loose pants or skirts, and simple tops or T-shirts for girls.

Best Place to Meet Guys/Girls

The best place to meet guys and girls at Wash U is through extracurricular activities (clubs, sports, artistic or religious organizations). The follow-up, of course, takes place everywhere else—at frat parties, in Ursa's or the Hilltop Café, in Bowles Plaza, etc. First getting to know girls/guys in a more intimate setting, where you share an interest, later allows for casual encounters in the popular places of campus life: the Quad, parties, the library, the eateries, and so forth.

Did You Know?

Top Three Places to Find Hotties:
1. The Quad
2. Off-campus parties
3. The piano practice rooms

Top Places to Hook Up:
1. The frats
2. Concordia Seminary (it's a beautiful walk, with vast lawns and romantic lighting)
3. Someone else's room on the floor
4. Under the arches at Brookings
5. Off-campus parties

Students Speak Out On...
Guys & Girls

> "I've found it a little tough to find hot guys at Wash U, but they're not all nasty either. It's just a little more work than I'd like."

Q "The guys always joke that **the girls are ugly because we're not a big state school**, but guys can be like that. I found there to be a lot of really cute guys on campus. The fraternities and sororities have formals, semi-formals, and date parties all the time, which you can be invited to even if you're not in one. The South 40 has a formal every year, and there are constantly parties on and off campus, which all make for good opportunities to meet people. Plus, there are a million organizations for every possible interest one might have, so meeting people isn't too much of a problem. Plus, almost all of the dorms are coed, and there is the phenomenon of the freshman dorm floor, where you would have to try not to make friends. I happen to be really shy, but I was immediately picked up by a group of fun people on my freshman floor that ended up being some of my best friends at school. In other words, dating isn't a problem."

Q "**Girls are not good-looking at Wash U**. They pale in comparison to other campuses—especially state campuses. There aren't that many beautiful women, and the ones that are have big heads because they're such hot commodities."

Q "**This isn't like Hawaii or Florida**; there are lots of smart people, but they're all really nice and fun. And there are cute guys, but sometimes you need to look a little harder (shh, don't tell anyone I said that!)."

Q "Well, I am a guy. I don't want to sound mean or anything, but for the sake of honesty, I can tell you that **the girls here are not too attractive**. I don't know much about the guys, but from the girls I've talked to, the guys are apparently good looking; but then, I can't really confirm that one."

Q "I'd say **students at Wash U are average** when it comes to attractiveness."

Q "I think we have a fairly attractive campus, but beauty is in the eye of the beholder, of course. **I've seen many a fine lad around the Quad, though**. Also, it seems the trend is that the younger classes just get hotter and hotter. Last year's freshman class—dang!"

Q "I'll speak for the guys and say that we have a pretty decent selection here. **There are a lot of different choices**—from Abercrombie guys, to sports, to artsy, to whatever—for whatever you might be into!"

Q "I've met a number of great guys, but mostly just as friends. I am dating a wonderful guy at the moment, so there are a few good-looking guys here. **The girls here aren't too catty** or anything. I have a number of girlfriends whom I can totally relate to and spend lunch breaks or time after class just sitting and talking to."

Q "**We have our share of partiers**, and people that stay home on the weekends and study, and then those that go in between. It just depends. There are lots of really cool people, though, from all over the country. It's funny how Wash U just becomes a melting pot in the Midwest."

The College Prowler Take On...
Guys & Girls

Considering the intellectual quotient of Wash U's undergrads, the kids here are surprisingly photogenic. This is partially because the highly athletic student population has a knack for staying in shape and keeping their bodies healthy. Guys and girls with flat abs and muscled legs can regularly be seen jogging near campus, lifting weights in the AC, and playing fast-paced ultimate Frisbee or soccer in the Swamp or Mudd field. Most people are slim, fit, and know how to dress to show it off (or undress, as the case may be).

There are plenty of attractive girls and guys to be found, it's just a matter of getting out and meeting them. Sexual relations at Wash U begin with the usual college immaturity and insecurity—awkward hookups, short-lived boyfriends and girlfriends. But overall, the student population is active and fun, and enjoys the company of the opposite sex (or the same sex, according to preference).

The College Prowler® Grade on Guys: C+

A high grade for Guys indicates that the male population on campus is attractive, smart, friendly, and engaging, and that the school has a decent ratio of guys to girls.

The College Prowler® Grade on Girls: C

A high grade for Girls not only implies that the women on campus are attractive, smart, friendly, and engaging, but also that there is a fair ratio of girls to guys.

Athletics

The Lowdown On...
Athletics

Athletic Division:
NCAA Division III

Conference:
UAA

School Mascot:
The Wash U Bear

Men Playing Varsity Sports:
234 (8%)

Women Playing Varsity Sports:
159 (5%)

Men's Varsity Sports:
Baseball
Basketball
Cross country
Football
Soccer
Swimming and diving
Tennis
Track and field

Women's Varsity Sports:
Basketball
Cheerleading
Cross country
Soccer
Swimming and diving
Tennis
Track and field
Volleyball

Intramurals:
Arm wrestling
Badminton
Basketball
Billiards
Bowling
Cross country
Flag football
Golf

(Intramurals, continued)
Inner tube water polo
Racquetball
Soccer
Softball
Swimming
Table tennis
Tennis
Track and field
Ultimate Frisbee
Volleyball
Wallyball

Club Sports:
Badminton
Crew
Cycling
Field hockey
Gymnastics
Ice hockey
Lacrosse
Roller hockey
Rugby
Sailing
Soccer
Table tennis
Tae Kwon Do
Ultimate Frisbee
Volleyball
Water polo (men's and women's)

Athletic Fields
Busyhead Track (track, recreation), Francis Field (track & field, football), Mudd Field (soccer, Frisbee), the Swamp (all-purpose, soccer, Frisbee), TAO Tennis Center, Kelly Field (baseball, IMs), Softball Field

Getting Tickets
A few sports events, like the women's basketball and volleyball games, occasionally involve a ticket purchase, but the vast majority of Wash U sporting events are free to the public.

Most Popular Sports
On the varsity level, the football and soccer teams have the largest presence on campus, but that presence is still pretty small. Women's volleyball and basketball are very successful teams, so they also draw large crowds. All of the IM sports are very popular, ultimate Frisbee and flag football in particular.

Overlooked Teams
A few teams at Wash U which don't always get a second look: the competitive ultimate Frisbee team that often plays other schools around the country; the relatively newly-formed rugby team which competes with local universities; and the sailing team, which competes in regattas all over the Midwest.

Best Place to Take a Walk:
Concordia Seminary, across from the South 40

Gyms/Facilities
Athletic Complex
The AC is the main sports facility on campus. It's most popular features are the weight room, which is often very crowded after 4 p.m. or so, the Olympic-size Millstone pool, and the basketball, volleyball, badminton, handball, racquetball, squash and tennis courts. The facility also offers athletic classes. It isn't a top-notch facility by any means, but it is big enough to accommodate many activities, and it provides equipment for a wide range of sports at no charge.

The South 40 Fitness Center

When the AC is closed, or seems too far away, the S40 Fitness Center is a nice alternative option. For a small annual fee, students have access to weight equipment and a large collection of exercise bikes and treadmills, as well as aerobics, kickboxing, and yoga classes. South 40 Fitness is located upstairs in Wohl Center.

TAO Tennis Center

Wash U's eight outdoor courts, located right in front of the athletic complex, are used by the tennis team throughout the year. But they are open to the general public at all other times and have lights so you can play at night.

The Swamp

Behind the sprawling lawn that usually serves as an ultimate Frisbee, football, or soccer field, stands a large outdoor basketball court with several hoops. On the other end of the Swamp lies a beach volleyball court with real sand.

Students Speak Out On...
Athletics

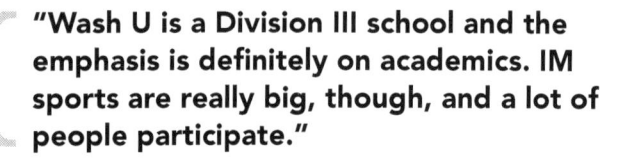

> "Wash U is a Division III school and the emphasis is definitely on academics. IM sports are really big, though, and a lot of people participate."

Q "Some varsity sports are bigger than others. I play on the soccer team, and we don't get very many fans. Volleyball and basketball are our two biggest varsity sports. We do have a football team, and they are pretty big, too, but volleyball and basketball get more fans because we usually win the title for those two sports. I also played IM coed softball my freshman year, and it was a blast! **We also have club sports which are in between IM and varsity,** if you want a little more competition."

Q "The school is Division III. **Sports are not huge, by any means**; however, the women's basketball team has been the national champs for several years in a row now. The women's volleyball team is also really good. IM sports are really popular. Every club and organization seems to have a team, and anyone can join. If you want to play, you can usually join a team even if you're not part of the organization. There's also what's known as club sports, which are somewhere between varsity and IM. They are like IMs, but they're for people a little more dedicated. They hold practices all the time. For instance, if you want to play a sport but don't have the time to play varsity or don't make the team, but you still don't want to play with people who may never have played before in their lives, you can do club sports."

Q "Women's varsity basketball is pretty big, and the swim team is really good. **A lot of kids play IM sports** and a lot of the dorms have floor teams and stuff."

Q "**I love going to basketball games**. Sometimes they can be very exciting, especially if we are having a good season."

Q "There are lots of opportunities. **Varsity sports are pretty big and fairly good**. Field hockey, lacrosse, swimming, some individual track events, basketball, squash—all are competitive on the national level, and some have several national titles. There are also club sports, which are sort of like varsity but officially a step below."

Q "**Varsity sports are very unimportant** at Wash U (I didn't even know when it was homecoming). IM sports are huge, though. So many students participate in IM sports. They're so much fun!"

Q "I didn't even know we had varsity athletics here. Truly, **sports are not big on campus at all**. I have not been to a single sporting event in my time here."

Q "**Sports are really not big at all at Wash U**. That's one thing I don't like here. There's not a lot of school spirit on campus. There are, however, lots of opportunities to play IM sports, especially Frisbee."

Q "**No one really goes to the football games here**—it's just not a very big thing. Girl's basketball is kind of big; they've done really well in the past. A lot of people get involved in IM or club sports, also, and really enjoy them. There are, like, a million of them. IMs are easy to organize and easy to get involved with, and club sports like girl's lacrosse and crew are also pretty popular."

The College Prowler Take On...
Athletics

The typical big-draw college sports, like men's football and basketball, struggle for any kind of following at Wash U—bleachers for these events are, at best, peppered with loyal fans and the occasional girlfriend or boyfriend. Most other sports suffer the same fate. For two sports only, turnout is never a problem. The women's volleyball team, which has won eight national championships since 1989, and the women's basketball team which won four consecutive NCAA titles (1996-2000), both enjoy a contingent of die-hard fans and draw big crowds for their high-quality matches.

The real sports scene at Wash U is recreational. Thousands of students participate in the intramural leagues, and it's fair to say that Wash U is an exceptionally athletic campus when compared to its peers. The annual Residential College Olympics on the South 40 are only one of many major amateur sporting events throughout the year, including several 5K runs, year-long IM leagues, and intra-fraternity competitions. There are also a number of club sports, often slightly more competitive than IM leagues, that provide a middle-ground between recreational sports and varsity. The running club is populated by former high-school long-distance stars, the sailing club competes at national regattas against top state-schools, the crew club practices every morning before class . . . the list of organizations is very long. Athletic students, in any case, will not wilt for lack of ways to stay in shape.

B-

The College Prowler® Grade on
Athletics: B-

A high grade in Athletics indicates that students have school spirit, that sports programs are respected, that games are well-attended, and that intramurals are a prominent part of student life.

Nightlife

The Lowdown On...
Nightlife

Club and Bar Prowler:
Popular Nightlife Spots!

Club Crawler:

Clubbing is not a huge part of the St. Louis nightlife. Beer and blues are more predominant than reflective pants and techno. Among the clubs that do exist, most are located together on the Washington Avenue strip downtown. Here are the best addresses there and around.

Miso

www.misolounge.com
16 N Meramec Ave., Clayton
(314) 863-7888

For a totally transforming experience, just walk through the banal ground floor of Miso and head downstairs. The spacious lounge and bar area hidden below are set in glowing hues of low blue, and the basement's 4,000 square feet (the space served as a bowling alley after World War II) immediately creates a rich and

(Miso, continued)

welcoming atmosphere. Purple and tan plush couches, armchairs, and love seats make loungers want to sink in and stay a while. The cuisine at Miso is surprisingly on par with the gorgeous surroundings. The sushi is excellent and goes down smoothly with their warm house-sake (or one of their eight other varieties of sake). Hip exotica and downbeat music pours softly over the speakers, but Wednesday through Sunday nights, Miso entertains a club crowd, bringing in DJs to spin the latest house music for the photogenic crowd.

The Pageant

6161 Delmar Blvd.

(314) 726-6161

www.thepageant.com

The Pageant is a large music venue with an open main floor with plenty of standing room and some seating on a first-come-first-serve basis. There is also an upstairs balcony with limited space, as well as the 21-and-over Halo Bar which serves drinks during shows. The Pageant has seen acts such as Collective Soul, Vertical Horizon, Steely Dan and the Doobie Brothers, and Ben Folds. Tickets are purchased through Ticketmaster.

Bar Prowler:

As soon as Wash U students turn 21, bars tend to become a big attraction—so much so that on the weekends, a few popular bars feel like extensions of the frat houses. Below are some names to help you find the scene, or avoid it, if necessary.

Cicero's

6691 Delmar Blvd.

(314) 862-0009

www.ciceros-stl.com

Don't even attempt to read the lengthy beer menu at Cicero's, just ask for a recommendation from the able barmen and women and you won't be disappointed. Besides the bar, this Italian restaurant has a pair of decent pool tables, and a kicking music venue that hosts some of the best underground jam bands around, including Spooky Daly Pride, Jake's Leg, and Ekoostik Hookah.

Delmar Lounge

6235 Delmar Blvd.

(314) 725-6565

During the day, the Lounge is a classy place to catch a decent meal, and at night, to watch some excellent jazz acts. On the weekends, though, the bar becomes more of an extension of the frat scene than anything else, so plan accordingly.

The Hi-Pointe

1001 McCausland
(314) 781-4716
www.hi-pointe.com

A dive bar in the grand tradition, the place rocks from low ceiling to cramped wall. Five-dollar pitchers, and raw underground punk and rock bands every weekend make the place one of the best bars in the Wash U area.

Venice Café

1905 Pestalozzi
(314) 772-5994

A real gem, hidden deep in the thick of mid-town St. Louis, Venice Café is well worth the detour. Everything from the booze boat (an ornately decorated skiff transformed into a bar), to the vast patio, complete with bucket seat chairs and a koi pond, makes this place a full-on visual experience. The aural side isn't bad either—jam sessions, folk bands, and open-mics take to the small stage almost every night of the week.

VFW #3500

1717 South Big Bend Blvd.
(314) 645-9509

Don't look for the young, hip crowd to be hanging around the bar between a pair of Korean War vets, sipping a pint of Pabst Blue Ribbon or playing a game of Buck Hunter on the console. The VFW is a haven for real Missourians—pro-life, pro-NRA, pro-beer. But because of its dirt-cheap brews, it also attracts an occasional college group looking for a pre-party, or just a pitcher to sip on a weeknight. No pretensions, no drink specials, just beer and rugged veterans of foreign wars.

Other Places to Check Out:
The Backstage Bistro
BB's Jazz, Blues, and Soups
Blueberry Hill
The Big Bang
Broadway Oyster Bar
Fitz's
McGurk's
Mike Duffy's Pub and Grill
MP O'Reillys
Schlafly Tap Room
Trainwreck Ladede's Landing

Student Favorites:
Cicero's
Delmar Lounge
Venice Café

Best Music Venues:
Mississippi Nights
The Pageant

Bars Close At:
1 a.m. in the county, 3 a.m. in the city

Local Specialties:
Budweiser
Busch

Primary Areas With Nightlife:
The Central West End
Laclede's Landing
The Loop

Cheapest Place to Get a Drink:
VFW on Big Bend

Favorite Drinking Games:
Beirut (aka beer-pong)
Card Games (a$$hole)
Century Club
Quarters
Power Hour

Useful Resources for Nightlife:
www.digitalcity.com/stlouis
www.riverfronttimes.com

What to Do if You're Not 21

The Grind
56 Maryland Plaza, Central West End
(314) 454-0202

The Grind is located right on the edge of the neighborhood—"the St. Louis Greenwich Village." The Grind looks like a bar on the weekends, since it's packed inside and out, and the crowd is hip and attractive. It's actually a coffee house, though, so students who are 18-and-over are certainly welcome. You can either chill on the big patio and sip an iced coffee or mug of tea, lounge inside on the comfy sofas, or play a game of pool or foosball.

Mississippi Nights
914 N 1st St.
(314) 421-3853
www.mississippinights.com

Some of the shows here are 21-and-over only, but most just require a small surcharge. And it's worth it, because this is one of the best venues in St. Louis. You can see all kinds of music—jazz, rock, blues, jam bands. John Scofield, Leftover Salmon, Ozomatli, and G. Love and Special Sauce have all been recent visitors.

Tropicana Lanes
7960 Clayton Rd.
(314) 782-0282

Sometimes an 18-and-over club or bar just isn't fun when you're surrounded by older people with drinks, so why not just do something different? Tropicana has 52 lanes of bowling, but there's plenty of other things to keep you busy: pool tables, video games, a thuggish Friday night crowd, and pitchers of beer, if someone has a decent fake ID (or a real one).

WILD
WILD (Walk In Lay Down) is an all-day festival at Wash U, thrown at both the beginning and the end of the school year for students of all ages. Events include concerts, games, raffles, student performances, and free food. To see which bands will be performing the next scheduled dates, visit the production company Team 31's Web site: *team31.wustl.edu*

House Parties

House parties are huge at Wash U. There will inevitably be a few happening every weekend in the University City apartments, and they can be a blast. Most will have a keg, and cups are free, but if you're thirsty, bring your own booze, too, because these things sometimes get so packed you can't move past the foyer. The best way to find out about house parties is just to ask people what they're up to on a weekend evening, and inevitably word gets out. Many parties are associated either with fraternity members or with a tight-knit organization like the sailing club or KWUR.

Frats

See the Greek section.

Students Speak Out On...
Nightlife

"There are lots of bars on the Loop that are cool. Not many people go to clubs—we are bar fans at Wash U. As a freshman, I didn't go to bars much, but last year I went a few times. Most of the time, there's already tons going on around campus so there's really no need to go to a bar."

Q "There are a number of bigger clubs in town, but it is usually **easier to find some sort of party or activity on campus**. There are a number of student groups that put on giant dance parties throughout the year, and those are always packed. There's also a party/concert/festival put on each year called WILD by a group called Team 31. WILD happens once a semester and it is a day-long festival where the school brings in a big-name band to perform. WILD is the biggest event at the school: there's free food, and lots of drinking. When I was there, we had bands like They Might be Giants, G Love and Special Sauce, the Roots, De La Soul, Eve 6, Outkast, and Crazy Town."

Q "Most of the clubs and bars are downtown and in the Central West End (about a fifteen- and five-minute drive, respectively). **Lots of people take cabs to these places**. You can also always get a ride from someone with a car, or take the subway."

Q "I can tell you this: **you probably won't be going to any clubs or bars off campus during your freshman year**. It is extremely easy to get drinks on campus at frat parties and such. The school is pretty lenient about it."

Q "A lot of times, **we all actually party on campus—either in the dorms or on Fraternity Row**. Also, many people party at private off-campus apartment parties. But some clubs and bars that students do tend to frequent are Blueberry Hill (they are very strict about ID, so it's just for the 21-and-over crowd), Mike Duffy's (apparently they don't card there), and many others. The more time I spend off campus, the more I discover."

Q "I've never been to any of the bars or clubs around town. Well, I went to one for a concert, but it was open to all ages at that point. **Mississippi Nights has had some good bands come through**: Lifehouse and Five for Fighting. You can take the Metrolink downtown to get there (very accessible). Also, a bunch of bands come to the Pageant, which is only about a 15–20-minute walk from campus."

Q "**There's always something to do**—from frat parties, to off-campus parties, to whatever you're into. I've never had trouble finding somewhere to drink or party."

Q "There's Blue Hill, Brandt's, Fitz's, the Halo Bar inside Pageant, McGurk's in Soulard, the Venice Cafe in Soulard, and the Delmar Lounge. Then you have the ever-famous over-packed Saint Louis University bars that have the run-of-the-mill penny-pitcher nights, and everyone in there is under 21. On the whole, though, it's pretty hard to get into most places with a fake ID. Especially anywhere on Delmar. Don't try it unless you have a really good fake or it's the summer and Wash U isn't in session. **The Duck Room in Blueberry Hill is an awesome place to hear live music**. Downtown, a lot of people go to the Landing on the river. The Big Bang is a great little piano bar that's become pretty fun, and Mississippi Nights is one of the best live music venues in St. Louis. There are a lot of gay and lesbian bars—three for lesbians. I hear it's a pretty good ratio (for guys) there."

The College Prowler Take On...
Nightlife

Wash U kids take their nightlife seriously. For the first couple of years, most like to stay on or around campus and enjoy the frat parties, sophomore suite parties, and off-campus house parties. Frat Row definitely attracts a crowd every weekend, although it's not everyone's scene. There are a few bars around town that don't card too hard, as well, so it's possible to start exploring before turning 21 (the VFW is a good place to start). With a real (or quality fake) ID, a lot more of St. Louis nightlife opens up. There are tons of blues bars, like BB's Jazz, Blues and Soups, and music venues that are more 21-and-over friendly than underage-friendly, like Mississippi Nights, the Pageant, and Broadway Oyster Bar are.

For people with more eclectic or refined tastes, St. Louis has some other options besides bars and parties. The Backstage Bistro is a classy jazz club downtown, which features top performers like Ahmad Jamal and Joshua Redman. Next door is the St. Louis Symphony, one of the best in the country, which performs every Friday and Saturday night during the season. There are also a few clubs downtown, for those with a taste for loud music and close quarters. Washington Avenue has a strip of interesting venues, and by keeping an eye on the flyers posted in the Loop, it's easy to find out about DJ events, the occasional rave (mostly for high school kids, though), and hip-hop parties.

B+

The College Prowler® Grade on
Nightlife: B+

A high grade in Nightlife indicates that there are many bars and clubs in the area that are easily accessible and affordable. Other determining factors include the number of options for the under-21 crowd and the prevalence of house parties.

Greek Life

The Lowdown On...
Greek Life

Number of Fraternities:
12

Number of Sororities:
6

Undergrad Men in Fraternities:
849

Undergrad Women in Sororities:
828

Fraternities:
Alpha Epsilon Pi
Beta Theta Phi
Kappa Sigma
Phi Delta Theta
Sigma Alpha Epsilon
Sigma Alpha Mu
Sigma Chi
Sigma Nu
Sigma Phi Epsilon
Tau Kappa Epsilon
Theta Xi
Zeta Beta Tau

Sororities:
Alpha Epsilon Phi
Alpha Phi
Chi Omega
Delta Gamma
Kappa Kappa Gamma
Pi Beta Phi

Other Greek Organizations:
Black Greek Council
Gamma Sigma Alpha
Intrafraternity Council
National Panhellenic Council
Order of Omega
Phi Lambda Psi
Women's Panhellenic Association

Multicultural Colonies:
Alpha Phi Alpha
Kappa Alpha Psi
Phi Beta Sigma
Omega Psi Phi

Did You Know?

Once a year, the fraternities build sets and prepare a series of skits to perform as part of Thurtene Carnival, **the nation's oldest and largest student-run carnival**.

Students Speak Out On...
Greek Life

> "Greek life makes up about 20 percent of the student body—it's not overwhelming, and all fraternity parties are open to everyone. Greek life is really a complement to the social life on campus, not a hindrance."

Q "Frats always have parties and they are open to everyone. It's not like only frat brothers and sorority sisters can go to parties. Personally, I did not join a sorority; **I didn't even rush—it's just not my style**. I do know girls who pledged, though, and so far they like it."

Q "I joined a sorority my sophomore year, but decided after a year that it wasn't for me. **A bit too much happiness and flowers for too many girls who didn't really know each other** but pretended they did anyway! But there are lots of people who really enjoy it. You can always check it out and decide if it's for you."

Q "Greek life is present, but it **does not dominate the campus**. About 20 percent of students here are Greek (myself included), and it is a good atmosphere, but the campus is very close-knit and friendly, regardless of who is Greek and who is not."

Q "Greek life does not rule the campus. However, **the fraternities are open to anyone for parties on the weekends**, not just sorority girls. No one at Wash U really cares if you're in a sorority or not, as everyone kind of recognizes the fact that it's not for everyone."

Q "About 20 percent of Wash U is Greek. **Most of the socially active people are in sororities or fraternities**. However, that is not to say that they dominate. I'd say they are a presence on and around campus. All parties are open, so that's not a problem. Most of the Greek organizations are very active in the campus and St. Louis communities by way of community service stuff."

Q "**Greek life absolutely is not the only thing going on** in the social scene. The sororities don't even have houses, so if typical sorority living is something you had your heart set on this is not the place to go. The frats are usually where the big parties are, simply because the entire house belongs to the frat as opposed to dorms, but no one judges based on whether or not people are in a frat or sorority."

Q "Some people think Greek life is a huge part of life here. I certainly do not. I knew before I ever went to college that I wouldn't want to be part of the Greek scene. **None of the sororities on campus have houses**. If you do not want to be part of Greek life, there are plenty of other things to keep you busy. In addition, if you just want to party and get a few drinks, there are always several parties every weekend which, from what I know, are open to any and all."

Q "**Greek life is in existence here, but it's not huge**. It does not dominate the social scene, and people who don't pledge usually don't feel out of the social loop. However, I have to say frat parties are the wildest and most popular type of partying that goes on around campus. Usually there are frat parties every weekend, and most of the people who party all the time usually attend. I don't personally party every weekend, but its fun to go every once in a while."

Q "Greek life is here, but it **doesn't dominate the social scene**. The parties are all open to everyone. We have delayed rush, so freshmen can't rush frats or sororities until the spring semester. That gives you the chance to meet lots of people and make friends before deciding if Greek life is for you."

Q "**Greek life at Wash U is fabulous**! I am a huge fan of Greek life. I definitely came to college thinking a sorority was the last thing I'd ever be a part of. I'm currently a very active member of Delta Gamma, and I absolutely love it. I definitely don't think it dominates the social scene, but it is a really nice scene to get involved with if you are interested. Pledging is just a fabulous way of meeting and bonding with a lot of people. I would recommend that anyone rush. If it's not your thing, though, that's cool, and you're in good company either way. It's not the only form of socializing on campus, and there's no pressure to join. Also, frat parties are usually open to everyone, regardless if you are Greek or not, and there is no cover charge to get into them."

Q "Greek life really isn't that dominant at Wash U; only about 20 percent of students here are Greek. **It's just a personal choice**. I didn't pledge and I still had tons of fun, but I had other friends who were Greek and they really enjoyed it. So it's kind of up to you; but, regardless of your choice, your social life will not suffer."

Q "**You don't have to be Greek to party** or meet people at Wash U. It's not at all exclusive either. I'm not Greek, but I'm an athlete and we all kind of form our own coed, giant fraternity/sorority sometimes. Plus, going to the Greek parties, you always see people you know, but there are always more people to meet, and it can be fun. Joining just means it's another good way to meet tons of people, but it's definitely not a necessity. If I had it to do over, I still wouldn't have rushed."

The College Prowler Take On...
Greek Life

The Greek scene is a popular resource for incoming freshmen at Wash U. It's a way to quickly find a group of friends, meet guys and girls, and find a set of ready-made activities and social events. The frats and sororities have mixers, crush parties, and semi-formals throughout the year, as well as other intra-Greek events that make them a tight-knit community on campus.

Deciding whether to join a fraternity or sorority comes up pretty quickly, since rush events begin in early September and bids are given out at the end of the first semester. Another option is to rush sophomore year, but few people actually do so. Nearly a quarter of the student body joins a fraternity or a sorority, and among the socially active, that percentage could represent almost half. Most students argue that the Greek scene does not dominate, though. There are plenty of other parties and social groups around, and not joining a fraternity or sorority doesn't constitute social suicide.

B+

The College Prowler® Grade on Greek Life: B+

A high grade in Greek Life indicates that fraternities and sororities are not only present, but have an active, highly-visible role on campus. Other determining factors include the variety of houses available and the respect the Greek community receives from the rest of the campus.

Drug Scene

The Lowdown On...
Drug Scene

Most Prevalent Drugs on Campus:
Alcohol
Caffeine
Cocaine
Marijuana
Mushrooms

Alcohol-Related Referrals:
48

Alcohol-Related Arrests:
3

Drug-Related Referrals:
18

Drug-Related Arrests:
7

Drug Counseling Programs

The Center of Chemical Abuse Prevention Education (CAPE) provides the Washington University community with information, education, brief assessment, and referrals with regard to alcohol and other drugs. Outside treatment options include self-help groups, long- and short-term outpatient programs, individual and group programs, and residential short- and long-term treatment programs. CAPE also provides assistance with re-entry into the university community following completion of an outside treatment program. All services are free and confidential. Call 726-4140 for an appointment or more information.

University Health Services

East Building, Room 3420

(314) 935-6666

Services: alcohol dependency assessments, drug counseling

Health Expert

Umrath Hall, Room 103

(314) 935-7386

bfoy@restech.wustl.edu

Betsy Foy is a Certified Health Educator, specializing in alcohol and other drugs. Referrals to St. Louis treatment centers are also available.

Counseling Services

Umrath Hall, Room 213

(314) 935-6695

Appointments with counselors who can help isolate the reasons a student abuses alcohol or other drugs and make referrals to treatment centers.

Students Speak Out On...
Drug Scene

> "The most popular drug on campus is weed. I don't really know much about harder drugs, but I have heard of a few people who use them, so I know they're present."

Q "At Wash U, **there's lot's of drinking**, a fair amount of pot, ecstasy is becoming more prevalent, and there are a few cases of people who do coke in their rooms. I think that drinking and drugs can always be found on college campuses, and while Wash U is certainly a fun place, it isn't really what you'd call a 'party school.' In other words, if drinking and drugs make up your scene, you'll be able to find it, but if you want nothing to do with it, it can be avoided."

Q "**If you want to smoke weed, you can do so**. That's really the only common drug available at Wash U. If you crave drugs, you can get them, and people rarely get caught. However, if you are caught with an illegal substance, they often come down hard."

Q "Seek and you shall find. But, in general, **if you want to avoid drugs, that's also very easy**. I personally never saw anyone doing drugs, but then I also tend to avoid that crowd."

Q "Other than pot, **drugs are really not a problem at Wash U**. I'm sure harder drugs are used, but I never see it. That's a plus, as far as I'm concerned."

Q "I'm not going to say a drug scene doesn't exist, but I would say **it's not a huge problem** here—or certainly no worse than at other universities. It's kind of your choice. If you want to avoid it, believe me, you can, but it's kind of up to you and your choice. Either way, your decision won't have a drastic effect on your social life."

Q "Like even the most conservative universities, **a fair number of students do experiment with marijuana** during their freshmen and sophomore years. However, use is typically limited to just experimentation, and most students either stop completely or smoke very little by their junior and senior years. As a general rule, people who use drugs regularly have trouble keeping up with the rigorous academic schedule."

Q "I don't know too much about the drug scene on campus. I know it's there, but no one pushes anything or tries to get you to do anything you don't want to do. **It's not like they're selling crack in the library**!"

Q "Drugs **aren't too big on campus, except for weed**. This isn't nearly as tolerated, but it could be worse. The worst punishment I've heard of happening was someone got kicked out of the dorms for the following year after a second warning for smoking weed."

The College Prowler Take On...
Drug Scene

Those who have no interest in doing drugs will find it easy to build a drug-free social life at Wash U. Within certain social circles, pot is considered common currency, but unless all of your friends are potheads it won't pose any social difficulties to the non-user. Some harder drugs are used on campus, but the harder they get, the fewer people use them. Mushrooms are pretty normal for regular pot users, while cocaine has a surprisingly large presence, especially among the fraternity social scene. Ecstasy, however, is virtually absent from campus.

For those looking to avoid drugs at all costs, one big tip is to request a room on a substance-free floor or dorm, since most of the non-substance-free dorms will inevitably have a few pot smokers, and they may end up across the hall from you. For parties, it will be difficult to avoid drugs altogether, since petty drugs are a mainstay at frat parties, as well as off-campus events. When confronted with drugs, all you have to do is remember the sage advice of our former-first lady, Barbara Bush: "Just say no."

B-

The College Prowler® Grade on Drug Scene: B-

A high grade in Drug Scene indicates that drugs are not a noticeable part of campus life, drug use is not visible, and no pressure to use them seems to exist.

Campus Strictness

The Lowdown On...
Campus Strictness

What Are You Most Likely to Get Caught Doing on Campus?
- Drinking underage
- Public urination or indecency
- Parking illegally
- Making too much noise in your dorm
- Drinking legally (There are no open containers allowed on campus, except at official University functions, even if you are 21)
- Smoking pot
- Carrying alcohol across campus
- Mooning prospective students
- Streaking
- Trying to use a fake ID at an event with alcohol

Students Speak Out On...
Campus Strictness

> "The Wash U police tend to think that we are adults and can make our own decisions. I'd say they are fairly lax. You have to be doing something really bad to get into any kind of trouble with the police."

Q "They really are not too strict about that. They only care if its a beer can, but if it's in another type of glass, they won't check. The only thing they make you do is pour it out, throw it away, and a few give you the option of chugging it as long as it's disposed of. With drugs, they are a bit more strict. **If you're doing hard drugs, you can be arrested or thrown off-campus**, but with weed they usually just take your piece and your stash. It's a very liberal campus, from my point of view."

Q "When I was a freshman, **there were practically no rules** at all. The campus policy was basically, do what you want, act mature, and we won't bother you. Eighteen-year-old freshmen could be seen walking casually across campus with a can of beer in each hand. However, things have gotten more and more strict throughout the years. As long as the alcohol doesn't leave your room, you wont get in trouble (underage or not). There's drinking at the frat parties, but no one ever IDs you, and I've never heard of anyone getting in trouble. Basically, if you're of-age and drinking, no one cares. If you're underage, you just can't be in a public area. No one will search your room, no one will even bother you if they see you sitting in your room drinking (as long as you're not acting like an idiot). The policies change and become a little more strict every year, so don't hold me to this. But compared to other colleges, Wash U is the most lenient."

Q "The Wash U campus is **very laid-back about drugs and alcohol**. Basically, the rule is that if alcohol is in your room, the RAs can't do anything about it. If you have it in the hall, then theoretically they can write you up, but I've never seen that happen. With drugs, as long as you are in an environment where no one is around, like a closed room with the window open, you should be fine. After all, we are basically owned by Anheuser-Busch."

Q "**The police at Wash U are pretty cool about drinking**. Anheuser-Busch built almost half of our school so we have a very wet campus. Alcohol is allowed in all the dorms and at all the parties on campus. The only thing you're not supposed to do is carry open containers around campus."

Q "Honestly, **as long as you're acting like an adult, Wash U will treat you like one**. If you're drinking or doing drugs in your room and being cool about it, most likely no one will stop you or care. However, if you're waving beer cans around and peeing on buildings, you'll most certainly get in trouble. This is understandable. They do mind drugs more than drinking, but be careful and respectful and I don't think you'll get in trouble. There's not really big pressure to drink and do drugs on campus. If you want to, that's cool; if not, that's cool, too. I do, however, even if you don't drink, speak against living in a substance-free dorm. The kids there tend to be kind of weird and antisocial. Live in a normal dorm, and if you choose not to drink, no one will care or give you crap about it."

Q "While the drug policy is zero-tolerance, **the University does understand that some students will drink**. The administration focuses on maintaining a safe, respectful environment, rather than trying to break up every party with underage drinking. As a general rule, you will not get in trouble for drinking in your room, but if you vandalize or disrespect other students while you're drunk, may God help you."

Q "Wash U treats you like an adult. The legal drinking age is 21, so keep that in mind, but what you do in your own room, house, etc. is kind of up to you. **Your resident advisors are not going to thoroughly search and check every room**, but if there is a problem or something, they will step in and officiate. So, I'm not saying you won't or can't get into trouble, but it's kind of your choice to be responsible and everything."

Q "Wash U's drinking policy is that **they treat everyone as an adult until you give them reason to treat you otherwise**. If you are seen with an open container on campus (outside of your room) and are underage, they will ask you to dump it out. It may seem pretty lax, but we really don't have many problems. I think that since they don't hound you for drinking and students don't have to try to smuggle in alcohol, the thrill of it goes down a little bit and people tend to behave a little better."

Q "**No open containers on campus**! If you get caught smoking in your dorm, sometimes they write you up, sometimes they don't. There was just a big controversy about pot on campus, but I don't really know what came of it. As long as you're smart, they can't catch you. That's my rule. I think the frats—or at least some of them—just went dry, but there are ways around that.

The College Prowler Take On...
Campus Strictness

The nature of campus strictness has subtly, but noticeably, changed in the last few years at Wash U. A new, more severe alcohol policy was introduced last year, and campus police seem more vigilant about catching students breaking little rules around campus (playing Frisbee golf with beer, for example). Even still, it remains a laid-back campus, and as students point out, if you behave like an adult, the University will treat you as such. Basically, anything that you do in private that doesn't blatantly violate the law or disturb the peace is tolerated. The University obviously does not condone drug use and underage drinking, but they essentially leave it to the students to make their own decisions about that—as long as those decisions don't affect the health or tranquility of others.

On the other hand, in the event that someone repeatedly and blatantly steps over the line in some respect, the University has no mercy. Last year, one suite became well known for loud and frequent drug use and, after receiving several warnings to no effect, was raided by campus police, ejected from the residential college, and had several of its residents placed on academic probation. It just goes to show that while the rules are, usually, barely felt on campus, if you go a little too far, they can become quite tangible.

The College Prowler® Grade on
Campus Strictness: B+

A good grade in Campus Strictness means an overall lenient atmosphere on campus, and that rule-enforcement is not overwhelmingly present. The poorer the grade, the more strict the campus.

Parking

The Lowdown On...
Parking

Approximate Parking Permit Cost:
$365–$820 per year, depending on the location

Parking and Transportation Office:
(314) 935-5601
parking.wustl.edu

Student Parking Lot?
Yes

Freshmen Allowed to Park?
No

Common Parking Tickets:
Expired Meter: $10
No Parking Zone: $20–$25
Parking Without a Permit: $25
Handicapped Zone: $50
Fire Lane: $20

Parking Permits

Faculty and grad students both receive priority selection for parking permits.

Parking permits come in several different varieties—Yellow (student parking), Red (priority parking), Blue (dorm lots only), and night/weekend. There are also evening passes for commuters, as well as monthly and daily passes for visitors or those who will have their car on campus for only a short time.

Warning

If you accumulate three or more parking tickets, you'd better watch out! Your car will get this nice bright orange sticker (very hard to peel off) that marks you as "on the verge"—that is, if you acquire another parking violation, your car will be towed and only returned after paying a mammoth fee.

Did You Know?

Best Places to Find a Parking Spot
The Whitaker BME parking lot

University Circle in front of beautiful Brookings Hall (It's 30-minute parking, but who's checking?)

Along Forsyth Boulevard, next to the meters

Brookings Drive

Good Luck Getting a Parking Spot Here!
In front of Mallinckrodt

Students Speak Out On...
Parking

> "You can't have a car freshman year, but I don't think parking at Wash U is too big of a problem. Sometimes you might have to look a little harder to find a spot, but it's no worse than what you'd see at a shopping mall."

Q "Parking, I admit, is a pain in the butt. **Permits are expensive** (several hundred dollars per year), and freshmen aren't even allowed to have cars (although some clever freshmen are able to get upperclassmen to buy them a permit under their name). While this sounds annoying at first, you really don't need one. As a freshman, almost everything you want is on campus, and campus is small enough that everything is within walking distance."

Q "It's **not too terribly hard** to find parking spots on South 40. On main campus, it's definitely more of a challenge. There is also kind of a large fee to get a parking sticker for the year. As a careless junior, I can't tell you for sure how much it is. You absolutely don't need a car, though—the shuttle service is real good. Or you can just make older friends and hit them up for rides."

Q "Parking sucks and **freshmen can't have cars**. They did build an extension to one of the parking garages a few years ago, though, which relieved some of the problem."

Q "**Parking can be a hassle**, but everything is close enough to easily walk. Even students who live off campus are usually close enough to walk to their classes and student group meetings."

Q "When you move off-campus, most of the apartments are in walking-distance from campus, so **having a car isn't necessary**. Of course, it's always nice to be able to get away when you need to and drive around. There's an above-ground metro system in the city, as well. There are also campus buses that run regularly to different areas off campus (the grocery store, the mall, etc). And at night, there's a campus shuttle service where you can call a special number and tell the operator where you are, then they come and pick you up and drop you off wherever you want to go. It's totally free and really convenient when you feel lazy! Most of the drivers are other students."

The College Prowler Take On...
Parking

While there isn't much of an excuse to drive to campus every day (except for those few students who actually live far from the Hilltop), when it becomes necessary, parking offers few major difficulties. It's best to avoid the main parking lot next to Mallinckrodt and the psychology building, though. Even if you find a spot there, without a parking permit you are guaranteed to receive a ticket in under 90 minutes. Parking permits cost way more than they should, but they remain reasonable compared to many campuses. Students can choose permits for the dorms, main campus, and restricted parking spots.

Besides the official parking lots, there are a number of spots to be had with coin-operated meters, and it's feasible to get by parking once in a while without a permit (especially when you calculate that it would take more than 30 expired-meter tickets to equal the price of a parking pass!). For example, the gorgeous, tree-lined street leading to Brookings Hall has several spots, as does Forsyth Boulevard, right beside main campus. Still, the least stressful way to get to campus is to walk or bike. The colder and the wetter it is, the more the cars come out, and the more difficult it becomes to find a spot.

B-

The College Prowler® Grade on
Parking: B-

A high grade in this section indicates that parking is both available and affordable, and that parking enforcement isn't overly severe.

Transportation

The Lowdown On...
Transportation

Ways to Get Around Town:

On Campus

Wash U Transportation Services
transportation.wustl.edu
(314) 935-5600 (Shuttle Service)
Shuttle Hours: 7 a.m.–7:30 p.m.
(314) 935-7777 (Escort Service)
Escort Hours: 8 p.m.–1:50 a.m. or 3:50 a.m., depending on the pick-up location

Public Transportation

The Metrolink and Metrobus
(314) 231-2345
www.metrostlouis.org

An above-ground metro that runs to most key locations in the downtown area and to Lambert International Airport but not much else. Tickets cost $1.65, and the Metrolink runs until around 1:30 a.m. on weeknights and 1 a.m. on weekends. The Metrobus runs throughout St. Louis and accepts the same tickets as Metrolink.

➜

Taxi Cabs

Ace Cab
(314) 423-2300

County Cab Co.
(314) 993-8294

Laclede Cab Co.
(314) 535-1162

Yellow Cab City Service
(314) 361-2345

Yellow Cab County Service
(314) 991-1200

Car Rentals

Alamo
Local: (314) 428-1405
National: (800) 462-5266
www.alamo.com

Avis
Local: (314) 426-7766
National: (800) 230-4898
www.avis.com

Budget
Local: (314) 423-3000
National: (800) 527-7000
www.budget.com

Dollar
Local: (800) 800-3665
National: (800) 800-4000
www.dollar.com

Enterprise
Local: (800) 325-8007
National: (800) 736-8222
www.enterprise.com

Hertz
Local: (314) 588-9431
National: (800) 654-3131
www.hertz.com

National
Local: (314) 426-6272
National: (800) 227-7368
www.nationalcar.com

Best Ways to Get Around Town

A bike

Convince a friend to chauffeur you

The Metrobus

The Metrolink

Your own two feet

Ways to Get Out of Town:

Airport

Lambert International Airport
(314) 426-8000

Lambert International Airport is 6 miles and approximately 20 minutes driving time from Wash U.

Airlines Serving St. Louis

American Airlines
(800) 433-7300
www.aa.com

America West/US Airways
(800) 428-4322
www.usairways.com
www.americawest.com

Continental
(800) 523-3273
www.continental.com

Delta
(800) 221-1212
www.delta-air.com

Northwest
(800) 225-2525
www.nwa.com

Southwest
(800) 435-9792
www.southwest.com

(Airlines, continued)

TWA
(800) 221-2000
www.twa.com

United
(800) 241-6522
www.united.com

How to get to the Airport

A cab ride costs about $25.

Metrolink costs about $3, and there's a station on Delmar Boulevard near campus.

Ridefinders, will help you find someone going to the airport so you can carpool.
Call (800) 847-7433 or visit www.ridefinders.org

Campus Parking & Transportation Services and Residential Life have also developed a shuttle plan for students to get to the airports during some holiday and other campus breaks. Students can call Parking Services (314) 935-5601 for ticket information, or visit their Web site at:
transportation.wustl.edu

Greyhound

St. Louis Greyhound Station
1450 N 13th St.
(314) 231-4485
www.greyhound.com

The Greyhound Bus Station is in downtown St. Louis, around 30 minutes away on the Delmar-Forsyth shuttle route.

Amtrak

St. Louis Amtrak Train Station
551 S. 16th St.
(800) 872-7245
www.amtrak.com

St. Louis's unsightly Amtrak station is located under Highway 40, in downtown St. Louis, behind the Krel Center at the 14th Street Exit

Travel Agent

Judy Peil Travel
7800 Bonhomme Ave.
(800) 626-2577

Students Speak Out On...
Transportation

> "Public transportation here isn't that great. Basically, it can take you downtown and to the airport. Wash U has shuttle service which will take you to the supermarket, shopping mall, movie theater, and some other places."

"The **metro is the cheapest form of transportation** and goes all over the city of St. Louis. However, there isn't a metro stop on campus, so you have to take a campus shuttle to get to the first stop. This is somewhat of a pain in the butt. Campus shuttle services are very convenient, though, for getting around places near campus."

"Wash U has a **great shuttle system** that can get you most places you'll need to go. We have a subway called Metrolink that goes downtown. You can walk to the nearest station or take the shuttle there."

"I think **public transportation is pretty decent** around here. Wash U has their own set of shuttles that take you to different places on campus (though I never actually used the shuttles for that purpose). The shuttles also take you to the grocery store, Target, and the Galleria (a decently sized shopping mall)."

"St. Louis is a very spread-out city. The Metrolink, a light-rail system, does offer access to downtown, though **most people prefer to drive their own cars**. For people without a vehicle, getting a ride from a friend or taking the University shuttle system is never a problem."

Q "**Transportation is really convenient here**. Wash U has a shuttle system that takes you to the Central West End, the Galleria, the grocery store and Target, the Loop, etc. When you hop on the one that goes to the Central West End, you can get off by the Metro link stop and take that into downtown St. Louis to go explore everything. So it's pretty easy to get around off campus. I would just recommend taking advantage of public transportation more than I have."

Q "The school has transportation that will get you many places on campus, so I've never really used public transportation. The Metrolink will take you to any place in STL that you want to go. Wash U also has a shuttle to the metro station, and I think **round trip tickets are cheap**, so that's nice."

The College Prowler Take On...
Transportation

Public transportation in St. Louis is not brilliant, by any means. The Metrolink (St. Louis's above-ground rail line) has recently been expanded to include a stop near campus, but it will still be a limited resource. Besides the Metrolink, St. Louis has a complicated bus service and no subway, which makes a car indispensable for full access to the city and the surrounding areas. The convenient Wash U shuttles that run to nearby supermarkets, shopping malls, and movie theaters makes up somewhat for this deficiency, but public transportation is one of St. Louis' major problems.

Further, St. Louis has a particularly spread-out geography. Interesting things to do are dispersed throughout a radius of several miles in the metro area, making access difficult without a car. Of course, everybody has friends with cars—even freshmen—so making some kind of quid pro quo arrangement with that friend might be a nice way to overcome St. Louis's shortcomings in the transportation arena and see what the area has to offer.

The College Prowler® Grade on Transportation: C+

A high grade for Transportation indicates that campus buses, public buses, cabs, and rental cars are readily available and affordable. Other determining factors include proximity to an airport and the necessity of transportation.

Weather

The Lowdown On...
Weather

Average Temperature:		**Average Precipitation:**	
Fall:	62°F	Fall:	3.34 in.
Winter:	27°F	Winter:	2.33 in.
Spring:	70°F	Spring:	3.91 in.
Summer:	88°F	Summer:	3.75 in.

Students Speak Out On...
Weather

> "If you don't like the weather in St. Louis, just wait 10 minutes—it's that unpredictable. August and September are usually hot, fall is really nice, December–February is cold (it snows about once-a-week), and March–May is pleasant."

Q "We have four seasons in STL. The winter seems freezing to me, but I'm from south Florida. **It snows some in the winter, but not tons**. The spring and fall are really nice, but in the summer it is extremely humid, which makes it feel like it's 150 degrees outside. That's not a huge issue, though, because students get there right at the end of the summer, so we don't have to suffer through much of that. Personally, I love it here."

Q "I'm not sure what kind of weather you're used to, but **weather in St. Louis is average**, I guess. It's really hot in the summer, and mildly cold in the winter (but it usually doesn't snow more than once or twice). I think it didn't even snow at all my senior year."

Q "Weather is beautiful in the spring and fall, **chilly in the winter**, and way too humid in the summer."

Q "**The weather here is totally crazy**. It could be 30 degrees one day and 65 degrees the next, but it's not super scary."

Q "The fall and spring are **beautiful and mild**, but be sure to pack some extra-warm clothes for the winter months."

Q "The weather **sucks about five months out of the year** because of grey skies and sloppy snow, but the spring is unbelievable. Depending on where you are from, you should be able to adapt."

Q "St. Louis weather is a little unpredictable. It's not really that cold in the winter, and **snow is only an occasional thing**. But sometimes it's just freaky—like 70 one day and 40 the next. But overall, it's not that bad. Still, coming from sunny California, it may seem a little cold."

Q **"The weather here is schizophrenic**! Seriously, you'll go from 80 degrees to 40 within the week. I've seen it! Usually, it's pretty moderate, though; it's nothing too extreme. There's not too much snow, and the heat is usually never excruciating."

The College Prowler Take On...
Weather

For reasons better explained by a qualified meteorologist (for example, local favorite Ben Able of 90.7 KWMU), St. Louis frequently experiences dramatic shifts in weather from one day to the next. Last spring, on more than one occasion, it snowed one day and was warm enough for T-shirts and shorts the next. That said, the pattern of seasons remains relatively constant. The range of conditions goes from quite cold in the winter (bring lots of fleeces, sweatshirts, gloves, a hat, and a winter coat), to unbearably hot and muggy in the summer.

Fall and spring, though, are two delightful seasons. Warm and sunny at first, fall tapers off into cool breezes, gorgeous foliage changes, and hazy golden sunsets. And spring in St. Louis is well worth the wait through the often agonizingly long winter. Trees and flowers bloom and blossom all over campus, temperatures reach warm but rarely unpleasant highs, and most importantly, students suddenly begin wearing less clothing than before. All of those pasty white bundles of overworked, sun-deprived students finally shed their layers and show off their occasionally sexy bodies.

B-

The College Prowler® Grade on Weather: B-

A high Weather grade designates that temperatures are mild and rarely reach extremes, that the campus tends to be sunny rather than rainy, and that weather is fairly consistent rather than unpredictable.

WASHINGTON UNIVERSITY IN ST. LOUIS
Report Card Summary

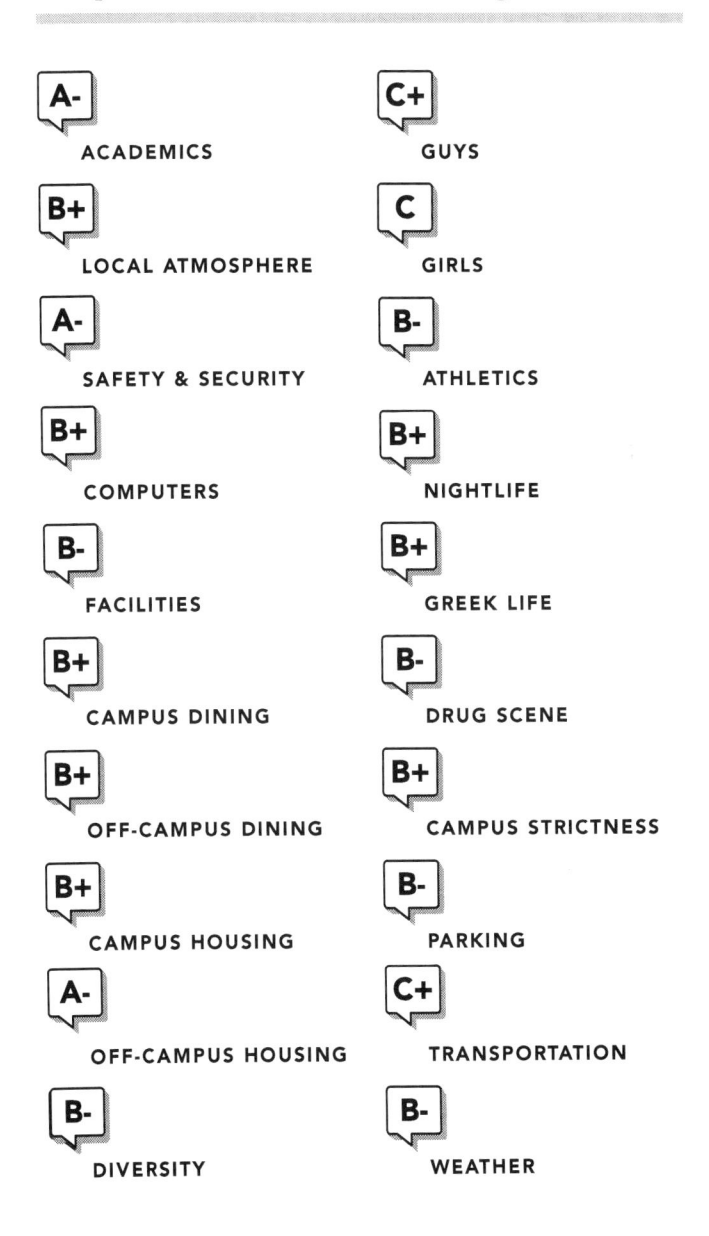

A- ACADEMICS

B+ LOCAL ATMOSPHERE

A- SAFETY & SECURITY

B+ COMPUTERS

B- FACILITIES

B+ CAMPUS DINING

B+ OFF-CAMPUS DINING

B+ CAMPUS HOUSING

A- OFF-CAMPUS HOUSING

B- DIVERSITY

C+ GUYS

C GIRLS

B- ATHLETICS

B+ NIGHTLIFE

B+ GREEK LIFE

B- DRUG SCENE

B+ CAMPUS STRICTNESS

B- PARKING

C+ TRANSPORTATION

B- WEATHER

Overall Experience

Students Speak Out On...
Overall Experience

"I wouldn't want to go anywhere else for college. So far, these two years have been awesome! I love Wash U so much and everyone I know who goes here loves it. It is a great place in a great location. This was the best decision I could have made. It's a great place!"

"I love Wash U, and **I've never regretted my choice to come here**. It was a really hard decision (as I'm sure you know), but I've had a fabulous time and I'm really sad to think I have to leave soon. The people here are just so nice and you just feel so included and like a family. Wash U is just a great school in so many ways!"

Q "**I had the best time of my life at Wash U** and I wouldn't have switched schools if they paid me. While I learned a lot from my classes (I was an English major), college was really an amazing time (as cheesy as it sounds) to learn about myself and to grow in all kinds of ways. I met amazing people, had the opportunity to participate in great activities, and overall just had a good time. One thing in particular that I really liked about Wash U was that the administration really worked well with the student body. In a lot of other schools (my high school, in particular), there is a feeling that the administration thinks it's better than you, wants to rule over you, and doesn't respect you. At Wash U, there isn't much sense of a controlling entity hovering over the student body. That isn't to say that it doesn't do it's job, but you feel respected and free to pursue your interests. Teachers respect you; they consider your ideas as opposed to preaching to you. Deans can be seen walking across campus and will be happy to sit down and have lunch with you if you need to talk."

Q "What I really liked about the school was its size. It was small, but not tiny. I always describe it as small enough that **you'll always recognize someone wherever you go**, but big enough that there will always be new people to meet. The campus is really pretty. They're constantly renovating. A lot of the buildings on campus look like modern castles. There are lots of trees but you're by no means living in the woods. The grass and flowers are all maintained very well. In general, it's pretty and comfortable. The atmosphere is friendly and cheerful."

Q "**I really am happy that I chose to attend Wash U**. I looked at some other schools, such as MIT, the University of Maryland, Tulane, and Carnegie Mellon, and Wash U was the best fit for me. The academics are very good, depending on what major and department you choose. Our chemistry and lab sciences are ranked very well, and they recently built a new lab building. Business, law, and pre-med programs are also very good."

Q "I think **everyone here contemplates transferring at some point**. Sometimes St. Louis gets old and I really wish I were somewhere else—out West, or at least somewhere more liberal. St. Louis itself is very conservative. Wash U exists in this weird little liberal bubble. It's actually a good experience, though; it makes you appreciate other places, I guess. I actually had to decide between Emory and Wash U. After visiting both, I decided Wash U was the place for me. Emory was beautiful, and I love Atlanta, don't get me wrong, but when it came down to the people, Wash U was much more welcoming and warm and genuinely interested in getting to know me as a person."

Q "I've had wonderful experiences since I've been here. **I don't wish I were anywhere else because I really think this is where I belong**. I've kind of made it my home. College is really what you make of it. Wash U has given me the opportunity to get involved, try new things, and meet a ton of people, in addition to offering me a wonderful education. I've had to work really hard (kind of difficult since I didn't study much in high school—but I do now). But all work and no play is definitely not the motto here!"

Q "I absolutely love Wash U! **It is a perfect school for many reasons**. It is not too small that you feel like you are not always meeting new people, yet not too big to feel like a number."

Q "Aside from being on an island surrounded by beautiful naked women, **I can't think of anywhere I'd rather be**."

Q "**In a word, Wash U is incredible**! I've met the most unbelievable people and have been able to receive a fantastic education. I've had some amazing experiences, and just more than anything, I am so pleased with my college decision. I have never once wished I was somewhere else. I love Wash U, and I think almost anyone else you talk to here would tell you the same."

The College Prowler Take On...
Overall Experience

Beyond the initial enthusiasm that so many students express for their overall experience at Wash U, a common subject of praise relates to the freedom that characterizes student life. In the academic sense, this translates into an ability to bend the rules, an encouragement to build things if they aren't already available, and support from the University for students who propose new and well-thought-out initiatives. Wash U is a young school, and the University is very much interested in channeling the energy and enterprises of its students into new traditions and organizations that can help shape its identity.

Not everybody likes Wash U from the outset (this author included). St. Louis can get dull, the academic life can become overwhelming, and the social scene will eventually feel a bit claustrophobic. But the quality of the faculty, the ease and relative affordability of life in St. Louis, and the receptiveness of the administration to student projects makes it a place where a motivated student can do anything he or she wants. In the last few years, three students have won Rhodes scholarships, one started a magazine for homeless people to sell on the streets, another started a fencing club, one worked for David Letterman, and another worked on the Pathfinder mission to Mars. For the one who learns to draw on the richness of the community and resources offered by the Wash U community and St. Louis, the sky is the limit.

The Inside Scoop

The Lowdown On...
The Inside Scoop

Wash U Slang:
Know the slang, know the school. The following is a list of things you really need to know before coming to Washington. The more of these words you know, the better off you'll be.

The AC – The athletic complex; the main sports facility on campus.

ArtSci – College of Arts and Sciences.

Blue Hill – A popular bar on Delmar; the full name is Blueberry Hill.

BME (or Whitaker) – The Biomedical Engineering Building on the east side of campus.

The Bunny – A startling, bizarre, centrally-located sculpture of an emaciated bunny, commonly used as a meeting place.

Center Court (also known as "CC") – The all-you-can-eat cafeteria in Wohl Center.

Cheap Chinese – Wong's Wok, a very affordable Chinese stand in the Market in the Loop.

Filmboard – Student film series, screening movies off campus on Thursday nights.

Floorcest – Engaging in sexual relations with a member of your dormitory floor.

The Gargoyle – The music venue in the basement of Mallinckrodt.

The Hilltop – The main campus, site of the majority of academic buildings.

The Loop – A shopping district next to campus.

Olin – The main library on campus.

Pre-Frosh – A visiting, prospective freshman.

Pre-School – A derogatory term for the John B. Olin School of Business.

The Quad – The big grassy area enclosed by Brookings Hall and Ridgley.

The Rat – The Rathskeller, once the campus bar, now a big Subway shop.

The Row – Fraternity Row, the fraternity dorm area.

Sexiled – To have access to one's room barred because of sexual activity inside.

South 40 – The residential campus, located across the street from the Hilltop Campus.

Stud Life – Short for *Student Life*, the independent school newspaper.

The Swamp – The big athletics area on the South 40, with a big grass field, beach volleyball courts, basketball courts, and hammocks.

WUPD (pronounced "woop-P-D") – Wash U Police Deptartment.

Things I Wish I Knew Before Coming to Wash U

- Don't take the maximum number of courses first semester (or any semester thereafter).
- Learn meditation so that you'll be chilled out and have everything in perspective when everyone around you is worrying about a Geo-Microbiology midterm.
- Get off campus as much as possible.
- There are a lot of superficial, snotty people here, but you can avoid them.
- The academic rules are never as strict as they seem (e.g., you can design your own major).
- That I should learn to cook for myself, not use the meal plan too often, and sell my points towards the end of the year.
- How to manage my time better.
- That it's more important to meet people in the first year than to get straight As.
- Take time off. Study abroad, or simply take a year to travel and make sure you know what you want to do with your education (after all, it's pretty expensive).

Tips to Succeed at Wash U

- Join a million clubs, be open and friendly, and meet lots of people. You can always decide later on what clubs to drop and what people you want to avoid.
- Don't be shy.
- When choosing between work and something fun, go with fun.
- Keep your eyes open for events on and off campus by reading *Student Life* and the *Riverfront Times*.
- Pick classes you actually will enjoy.
- Do a really good job on one major, rather than a shoddy job on two.
- Seems obvious, but read the assigned material before class, and discussions will become infinitely more engaging.

School Spirit

Rather than specifically expressing their pride as Wash U students, students like to show how proud they are to be members of their specific fraternity or sorority, residents of such-and-such dorm, writers for a newspaper, athletes on a team, and so forth. Every club/team/sorority/dorm/class/religious group has its own T-shirt, party, visor, or memorabilia of some kind, and people tend to define themselves more specifically along those lines. The only events at which Wash U students gather and celebrate their pride in unison are perhaps convocation, the men's and women's basketball games, and the women's volleyball games which are unique among sports matches in drawing a large attendance.

Traditions

Boxapalooza
Wash U isn't sponsored by Anheuser-Busch for nothing. Every year, student groups, including fraternities, KWUR radio station staff, and RAs, organize teams to compete in this very healthy relay event. Each runner must drink a beer following every lap of a race, until a case of beer is finished. Whoever manages to actually finish this event without puking should receive a medal of honor, although only the first three teams receive official recognition.

Dance Marathon
Participants dance for twelve hours straight to raise money for the Children's Miracle Network, which provides services for kids with cancer. The marathon commonly brings in professional dance groups, like the Rams cheerleaders, and includes other entertainment events. The event usually raises as much as $50,000 and includes 150–200 dancers.

EnWeek
The most unusual members of the University (yes, I'm referring to the engineering students) finally show their pride (and their pale, pasty faces) in spectacular fashion for one week in the spring semester. They stage all kinds of bizarre and cool events, including three-dollar pizza lunches and a popular torture event in which volunteer engineering students are duct-taped, feet off the ground, to one of the columns in the engineering complex.

Powder Puff
The Alpha Phi sorority stages a full-tackle football game between two teams entirely made of its own members. It gets good when conditions are muddy, since the game will essentially deteriorate into an all-girl mud-wrestling match. This brings out the shameless chauvinist in all guys who walk by.

Streaking the Row
On the first night of Frat Row's opening, fraternity and sorority members like to show what they're made of, literally. Since a number of fraternities have moved off of the Row, this tradition might slowly fade, but there's still a hard-core group that should keep the tradition alive.

Thurtene
The nation's biggest student-run carnival, Thurtene has all kinds of rides, a ferris wheel, funnel cake, a haunted house, and goofy skits written, produced, and acted out by members of Wash U fraternities and sororities. It's for the kids, but a great time for the people who organize it, too.

WILD
It stands for Walk In Lay Down, although We'll Imbibe Like Dubliners and Wash U Incited Licentious Drinking also fit the bill. Twice a year, the University pays for a top band/performer to play a free outdoor concert for the entire student body. Past stars have included Busta Rhymes, Talib Kweli, the Roots, Counting Crows, Jurassic 5, and the Black Eyed Peas.

Finding a Job or Internship

The Lowdown On...
Finding a Job or Internship

Career Center:

157 Karl Umrath Hall
324 Lopata Hall
120 Bixby Hall
(314) 935-5930
careers@wustl.edu
careers.wustl.edu
Hours: Monday–Friday
8:30 a.m.–5 p.m.
Umrath 157 is open until 8 p.m.
Monday–Tuesday

Services Available:

Campus Employment
Career Counseling
Career Workshops
Graduate School Advising
Online database of fellowship, internships, and scholarships at Placement Advising
The Resource Center

Advice

Don't expect too much help from the Career Center, or from anyone else on campus in your internship- or job-search. Few people find terrific internships or jobs through the Career Center database. Instead, be proactive and look for jobs outside of campus career resources. Look, for example, at *Monster.com*, or local newspapers and magazines.

Perhaps a better way to find internships is to go directly to the Web sites of employers that interest you and see if official internship opportunities exist. If not, you still might be able to create one by finding the appropriate person to talk to at the business in question and sending your resume and a convincing cover-letter to him or her. Many local newspapers, law firms, businesses, and entertainment organizations are eager to hire Washington University students as interns or part-time workers, so it's just a matter of presenting yourself well and asking. There are also numerous jobs to be found on campus, from challenging research positions with prestigious professors, to lifeguarding at the athletic complex pool.

Keep your eyes open for postings around campus and on the Wash U Web sites. The commercial area of the Loop also offers employment opportunities in its numerous restaurants and stores. Inquire with store managers about work opportunities at some of the cooler stores like Vintage Vinyl or Plowsharing Crafts.

Firms that Most Frequently Hire Graduates

Boeing Company, Edward Jones, IBM, Merrill Lynch & Company, SBC Communications

Salary Information

Starting salary of average Wash U grad: $55,066

Average 10-year alumni salary: $125,000

Alumni

The Lowdown On...
Alumni

Office:
Alumni House
6510 Wallace Circle, 63105
Box 1210
(314) 935-5200
alumni.wustl.edu

Services Available:
Lifetime e-mail forwarding

The Alumni House:
The Alumni House stands right across Forsyth from the Hilltop Campus and includes rooms for receptions, marriages, and alumni events. Not generally available for use by students, but you might be lucky enough to be invited to one of the receptions there, which are always very well catered.

Major Alumni Events

The biggest event for alumni is Reunion Weekend, which serves as the Reunion date for all classes. Reunions usually take place from May 20–22. Since new events are always evolving, you can find a complete schedule of events on the alumni Web site at *alumni.wustl.edu*.

Alumni Publications

WU Magazine

WU Magazine comes out four times a year, giving regular updates on research, University projects, and alumni news. The magazine is free to faculty and alumni.

Did You Know?

Famous Wash U Alumni

Jack Taylor (Class of '42) – Founder of Enterprise Rent-A-Car.

Michael Shamberg (Class of '66) – Producer; credits include *The Big Chill*, *A Fish Called Wanda*, *Get Shorty*, and *Out of Sight*.

Harold Ramis (Class of '66) – Writer/Director; credits include *Analyze This*, *Caddyshack*, *Animal House*, and *Ghostbusters* (in which he also starred as Egon).

Steve Fossett (Class of '68) – Explorer; holder of several sailing and speed records, and the first person to circumnavigate the globe solo in a hot-air balloon.

Cara Nussbaum (Class of '01) – star of *The Real World: Chicago*.

Student Organizations

Cultural
Anime Exploration Team
ASHOKA (Indian/South Asian Students Associations)
Asian American Association (AAA)
Asian Multicultural Council (AMC)
Association of Black Students (ABS)
Association of Latin American Students (ALAS)
Batsheva (Jewish Woman's Club)
Black Men/White Men: Breaking Down Barriers
Black Women/Jewish Women: Discovering Common Threads
Chabad Jewish Heritage Student Association
Chinese Students Association (CSA)
Connections (International Student Association)
Hawaii Club
Heisei Japan Club
Hong Kong Students Association (HKSA)
Russian Club
Singapore Studenst Association
Students Taking On Multicultural Pursuits (STOMP)
Taiwanese Students Association
Turkish Student Organization
Vietnamese Student Association

Entertainment
Campus Programming Council (CPC)
Cheerleading
Filmboard
Gargoyle Committee (programming for campus music venue)
Homecoming Steering Committee
Team 31 Productions (programming for WILD)
WashU Jive (dance team for sports events)

Government
Congress of the South 40 (CS40)
EnCouncil
Undergraduate Women in Business

Literary and Media
Eliot Review (arts and literature magazine)
Hatchet (Yearbook)
KWUR 90.3 FM
Spires (arts and literature magazine)
Student Life (main student newspaper)
WUTV: Washington University Television

Performance
All Student Theatre
Amateurs (coed a cappella)
Black Anthology
Cultural Diversity Players (CD Players)
Greenleafs (female a capella)
Mama's Pot Roast (improv comedy)
More Fools Than Wise (madrigal singing)
Mosaic Whispers (coed a capella)
Pikers
Staam (coed Jewish a cappella)
Stereotypes (eclectic a cappella)

Political
Amnesty International
College Democrats
College Libertarians (CL)
College Republicans
Conservative Leadership Association (CLA)
Green Action

Green Givens (sustainable living)
Sakina: A Palestinian Advocacy and Dialogue Group
Students for Choice
Students for Life
Wash U Students for Israel

Recreational
Breakdancing Club
Outing Club
Wash U Photography Association (WUPA)
Wash U Swing Society (WUSS)

Religious
Asian Christian Fellowship (ACF)
ATMA – Hindu Students' Association
Baptist Student Union
Campus Pagans
Catholic Student Union
College Central
Episcopal Campus Ministry
Harambee Christian Ministries (HCM)
Jewish Student Union
Latter-day Saint Student Association (LDSSA)
Lutheran Campus Ministry
Muslim Students Association (MSA)
Wesley Fellowship

Service
Alpha Phi Omega (APO) (coed service fraternity)
Beyond the Surface
Circle K
Dance Marathon
Feed St. Louis
Mental Health Outreach Program
Special Olympics
STONE Soup
Teach ESL
The Watch (housing for kids from troubled homes)
Wash U Locks of Love (hair-donation event)

Since Wash U's Student Organizations are constantly being updated, a complete list can be accessed at:
su.wustl.edu/general/groupresources

The Best & Worst

The Ten BEST Things About Wash U

1. WILD
2. Your freshman floor
3. Residential College Olympics
4. Frisbee in the Swamp
5. Study abroad
6. Chancellor Wrighton's good eye
7. Annual inter-sorority mud wrestling
8. *Dark Side of the Rainbow* at Filmboard
9. KWUR
10. Korean techno and glow-stick parties

The Ten WORST Things About Wash U

1. The price of tuition ($$$)
2. Snobby rich kids
3. The weather
4. Chancellor Wrighton's lazy eye
5. Graduation requirements
6. Teachers with heavy accents
7. Pre-meds
8. Pre-laws
9. Senior theses
10. 9 a.m. classes

Visiting

The Lowdown On...
Visiting

Hotel Information:

Near campus:
Best Western Inn at the Park
4630 Lindell Boulevard
(314) 367-7500
www.bestwestern.com
Distance from Campus:
1.5 miles
Price Range: $72–$80

Chase Park Plaza
212-232 N. Kingshighway Blvd.
(314) 633-3000
Distance from Campus:
2 miles
Price range: $189–$329

The Cheshire Lodge
6300 Clayton Rd
(314) 647-7300
www.cheshirelodge.com

(Cheshire Lodge, continued)
Distance from Campus: Less than a mile
Price Range: $112–$250

Holiday Inn – Forest Park
5915 Wilson Ave.
(314) 645-0700
www.holiday-inn.com
Distance from Campus:
2 miles
Price Range: $84–$110

Residence Inn by Marriott
1100 McMarrow
(314) 862-1900
marriott.com/residenceinn
(314) 862-1900
Price Range: $160–180

Sheraton Clayton Plaza Hotel
7730 Bonhomme Ave.
(314) 863-0400
www.sheraton.com
Distance from Campus:
2 miles
Price Range: $199–$370

Downtown:

Drury Inn – Convention Center
711 North Broadway
(314) 231-8100
(800) 378-7946
www.druryhotels.com
Distance from Campus:
8 miles
Price range: $99–$119

Radisson - Downtown
200 North 4th St.
(314) 621-8200
www.radissonadisson.com
Distance from Campus:
7 miles
Price Range: From $69–$209

Take a Campus Virtual Tour

tour.wustl.edu

The admission staff interviews most Mondays through Fridays throughout the year; call (314) 935-9650 or (800) 638-0700 to schedule a time.

Information Sessions

September through November: Monday–Friday
10 a.m.–11 a.m., 1:30 p.m.–2:30 p.m.,
Saturday 9:30 a.m.–10:30 a.m., 11 a.m.–12 p.m.

December through February: Monday–Friday 10 a.m.–11 a.m.

Campus Tours

September–November: Monday–Friday 11 a.m.–2:30 p.m., Saturday 10:30 a.m.–12 p.m.

December–February: Monday–Friday 11:00 a.m.

The University is closed December 24–25 and January 1–19.

Directions to Campus

Driving from the West
- Take I-70 East to Exit 238B on I-170 South.
- Follow I-170 South to the Delmar Blvd. Exit.
- Follow Delmar to Big Bend and turn right.
- Make a left onto Forsyth Blvd.
- The campus is visible on your left; make a left into any of the parking lots.

Driving from the North
- I-94 W via the exit, on the left, toward Chicago.
- Merge onto I-80 W (Portions toll).
- Merge onto I-55 S via exit number 126A toward St. Louis.
- I-55 S becomes I-64 W/US-40 W.
- Take the Clayton Rd./Skinker Blvd exit number 34B.
- Turn right onto S Skinker Blvd.
- Turn left onto University Circle.

Driving from the South
- Take I-55 N via exit number 277 toward Blytheville/Jonesboro.
- Take the I-270/I-255 exit number 196 toward Chicago/Kansas City.
- Take the I-270 W exit number 196B on the left toward Kansas City.
- Merge onto I-270 N.
- Merge onto I-44 E via exit number 5A.
- Take the Jamieson Ave. exit number 284A.
- Turn Left onto Jamieson Ave.
- Turn Left onto Arsenal St.
- Turn Right onto McCausland Ave (aka Skinker Blvd.).
- Turn Left onto University Circle.

Driving from the East
- Take I-76 W.
- Merge onto I-70 W via exit number 8 toward US-119/Columbus/Wheeling.
- Merge onto I-465 S via exit number 90.
- Take the I-70 W/I-70 E exit number 9A-B toward Terre Haute/St. Louis/Indianapolis.
- Merge onto I-70 W via exit number 9B on the left toward Terre Haute/St. Louis.
- Merge onto I-55 S via the exit- on the left- toward St. Louis.
- I-55 S becomes I-64 W/US-40 W.
- Take the Clayton Rd/Skinker Blvd. exit number 34B.
- Turn Right onto S. Skinker Blvd.
- Turn Left onto University Circle.

Words to Know

Academic Probation – A suspension imposed on a student if he or she fails to keep up with the school's minimum academic requirements. Those unable to improve their grades after receiving this warning can face dismissal.

Beer Pong/Beirut – A drinking game involving cups of beer arranged in a pyramid shape on each side of a table. The goal is to get a ping pong ball into one of the opponent's cups by throwing the ball or hitting it with a paddle. If the ball lands in a cup, the opponent is required to drink the beer.

Bid – An invitation from a fraternity or sorority to 'pledge' (join) that specific house.

Blue-Light Phone – Brightly-colored phone posts with a blue light bulb on top. These phones exist for security purposes and are located at various outside locations around most campuses. In an emergency, a student can pick up one of these phones (free of charge) to connect with campus police or a security escort.

Campus Police – Police who are specifically assigned to a given institution. Campus police are typically not regular city officers; they are employed by the university in a full-time capacity.

Club Sports – A level of sports that falls somewhere between varsity and intramural. If a student is unable to commit to a varsity team but has a lot of passion for athletics, a club sport could be a better, less intense option. Even less demanding, intramural (IM) sports often involve no traveling and considerably less time.

Cocaine – An illegal drug. Also known as "coke" or "blow," cocaine often resembles a white crystalline or powdery substance. It is highly addictive and dangerous.

Common Application – An application with which students can apply to multiple schools.

Course Registration – The period of official class selection for the upcoming quarter or semester. Prior to registration, it is best to prepare several back-up courses in case a particular class becomes full. If a course is full, students can place themselves on the waitlist, although this still does not guarantee entry.

Division Athletics – Athletic classifications range from Division I to Division III. Division IA is the most competitive, while Division III is considered to be the least competitive.

Dorm – A dorm (or dormitory) is an on-campus housing facility. Dorms can provide a range of options from suite-style rooms to more communal options that include shared bathrooms. Most first-year students live in dorms. Some upperclassmen who wish to stay on campus also choose this option.

Early Action – An application option with which a student can apply to a school and receive an early acceptance response without a binding commitment. This system is becoming less and less available.

Early Decision – An application option that students should use only if they are certain they plan to attend the school in question. If a student applies using the early decision option and is admitted, he or she is required and bound to attend that university. Admission rates are usually higher among students who apply through early decision, as the student is clearly indicating that the school is his or her first choice.

Ecstasy – An illegal drug. Also known as "E" or "X," ecstasy looks like a pill and most resembles an aspirin. Considered a party drug, ecstasy is very dangerous and can be deadly.

Ethernet – An extremely fast Internet connection available in most university-owned residence halls. To use an Ethernet connection properly, a student will need a network card and cable for his or her computer.

Fake ID – A counterfeit identification card that contains false information. Most commonly, students get fake IDs with altered birthdates so that they appear to be older than 21 (and therefore of legal drinking age). Even though it is illegal, many college students have fake IDs in hopes of purchasing alcohol or getting into bars.

Frosh – Slang for "freshman" or "freshmen."

Hazing – Initiation rituals administered by some fraternities or sororities as part of the pledging process. Many universities have outlawed hazing due to its degrading, and sometimes dangerous, nature.

Intramurals (IMs) – A popular, and usually free, sport league in which students create teams and compete against one another. These sports vary in competitiveness and can include a range of activities—everything from billiards to water polo. IM sports are a great way to meet people with similar interests.

Keg – Officially called a half-barrel, a keg contains roughly 200 12-ounce servings of beer.

LSD – An illegal drug, also known as acid, this hallucinogenic drug most commonly resembles a tab of paper.

Marijuana – An illegal drug, also known as weed or pot; along with alcohol, marijuana is one of the most commonly-found drugs on campuses across the country.

Major –The focal point of a student's college studies; a specific topic that is studied for a degree. Examples of majors include physics, English, history, computer science, economics, business, and music. Many students decide on a specific major before arriving on campus, while others are simply "undecided" until declaring a major. Those who are extremely interested in two areas can also choose to double major.

Meal Block – The equivalent of one meal. Students on a meal plan usually receive a fixed number of meals per week. Each meal, or "block," can be redeemed at the school's dining facilities in place of cash. Often, a student's weekly allotment of meal blocks will be forfeited if not used.

Minor – An additional focal point in a student's education. Often serving as a complement or addition to a student's main area of focus, a minor has fewer requirements and prerequisites to fulfill than a major. Minors are not required for graduation from most schools; however some students who want to explore many different interests choose to pursue both a major and a minor.

Mushrooms – An illegal drug. Also known as "'shrooms," this drug resembles regular mushrooms but is extremely hallucinogenic.

Off-Campus Housing – Housing from a particular landlord or rental group that is not affiliated with the university. Depending on the college, off-campus housing can range from extremely popular to non-existent. Students who choose to live off campus are typically given more freedom, but they also have to deal with possible subletting scenarios, furniture, bills, and other issues. In addition to these factors, rental prices and distance often affect a student's decision to move off campus.

Office Hours – Time that teachers set aside for students who have questions about coursework. Office hours are a good forum for students to go over any problems and to show interest in the subject material.

Pledging – The early phase of joining a fraternity or sorority, pledging takes place after a student has gone through rush and received a bid. Pledging usually lasts between one and two semesters. Once the pledging period is complete and a particular student has done everything that is required to become a member, that student is considered a brother or sister. If a fraternity or a sorority would decide to "haze" a group of students, this initiation would take place during the pledging period.

Private Institution – A school that does not use tax revenue to subsidize education costs. Private schools typically cost more than public schools and are usually smaller.

Prof – Slang for "professor."

Public Institution – A school that uses tax revenue to subsidize education costs. Public schools are often a good value for in-state residents and tend to be larger than most private colleges.

Quarter System (or Trimester System) – A type of academic calendar system. In this setup, students take classes for three academic periods. The first quarter usually starts in late September or early October and concludes right before Christmas. The second quarter usually starts around early to mid–January and finishes up around March or April. The last academic quarter, or "third quarter," usually starts in late March or early April and finishes up in late May or Mid-June. The fourth quarter is summer. The major difference between the quarter system and semester system is that students take more, less comprehensive courses under the quarter calendar.

RA (Resident Assistant) – A student leader who is assigned to a particular floor in a dormitory in order to help to the other students who live there. An RA's duties include ensuring student safety and providing assistance wherever possible.

Recitation – An extension of a specific course; a review session. Some classes, particularly large lectures, are supplemented with mandatory recitation sessions that provide a relatively personal class setting.

Rolling Admissions – A form of admissions. Most commonly found at public institutions, schools with this type of policy continue to accept students throughout the year until their class sizes are met. For example, some schools begin accepting students as early as December and will continue to do so until April or May.

Room and Board – This figure is typically the combined cost of a university-owned room and a meal plan.

Room Draw/Housing Lottery – A common way to pick on-campus room assignments for the following year. If a student decides to remain in university-owned housing, he or she is assigned a unique number that, along with seniority, is used to determine his or her housing for the next year.

Rush – The period in which students can meet the brothers and sisters of a particular chapter and find out if a given fraternity or sorority is right for them. Rushing a fraternity or a sorority is not a requirement at any school. The goal of rush is to give students who are serious about pledging a feel for what to expect.

Semester System – The most common type of academic calendar system at college campuses. This setup typically includes two semesters in a given school year. The fall semester starts around the end of August or early September and concludes before winter vacation. The spring semester usually starts in mid-January and ends in late April or May.

Student Center/Rec Center/Student Union – A common area on campus that often contains study areas, recreation facilities, and eateries. This building is often a good place to meet up with fellow students; depending on the school, the student center can have a huge role or a non-existent role in campus life.

Student ID – A university-issued photo ID that serves as a student's key to school-related functions. Some schools require students to show these cards in order to get into dorms, libraries, cafeterias, and other facilities. In addition to storing meal plan information, in some cases, a student ID can actually work as a debit card and allow students to purchase things from bookstores or local shops.

Suite – A type of dorm room. Unlike dorms that feature communal bathrooms shared by the entire floor, suites offer bathrooms shared only among the suite. Suite-style dorm rooms can house anywhere from two to ten students.

TA (Teacher's Assistant) – An undergraduate or grad student who helps in some manner with a specific course. In some cases, a TA will teach a class, assist a professor, grade assignments, or conduct office hours.

Undergraduate – A student in the process of studying for his or her bachelor's degree.

ABOUT THE AUTHOR

Dan Carlin was born to write this guide. Raised just two blocks from Washington University, at age five he began gathering notes and conducting interviews for the College Prowler guide he was certain would one day bear his name.

A recent graduate in political science, Carlin is now a staff writer for *Desert Post Weekly* in Palm Springs, CA. He would like to thank his roommates, friends, cats, parents, and survey subjects for their help in putting the guide together, and he extends his eternal gratitude to the College Prowler team for hiring him.

He can be contacted for more information at authors@collegeprowler.com.

The College Prowler Big Book of Colleges

Having Trouble Narrowing Down Your Choices?
Try Going Bigger!

BIG BOOK OF COLLEGES '09
7¼" X 10", 1248 Pages Paperback
$29.95 Retail
978-1-4274-0005-5

Choosing the perfect school can be an overwhelming challenge. Luckily, our *Big Book of Colleges* makes that task a little less daunting. We've packed it with overviews of our full library of single-school guides—more than 280 of the nation's top schools—giving you some much-needed perspective on your search.

College Prowler on the Web

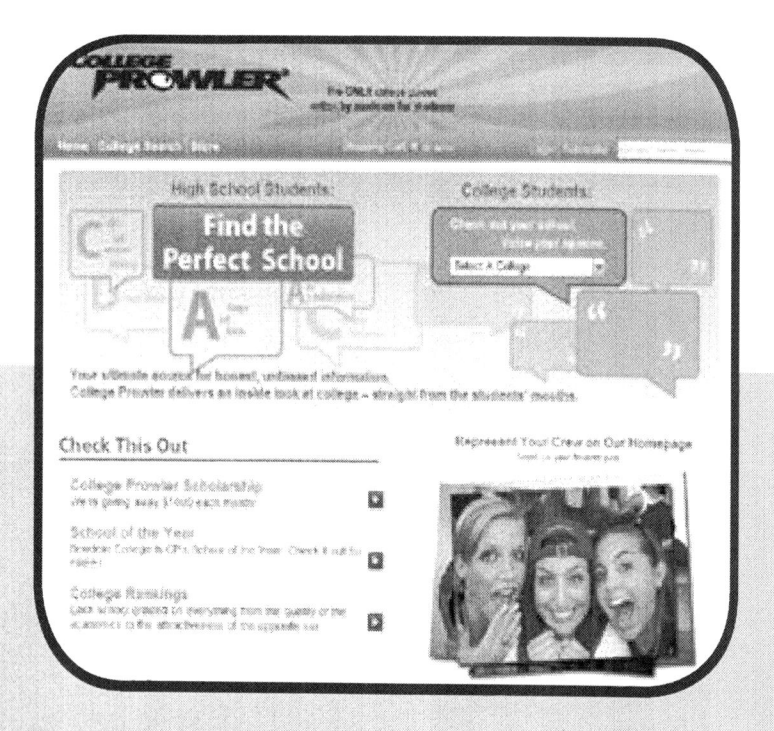

Craving some electronic interaction? Check out the new and improved **CollegeProwler.com**! We've included the COMPLETE contents of more than 250 of our single-school guides on the Web—and you can gain access to all of them for just $39.95 per year!

Not only that, but non-subscribers can still view and compare our grades for each school, order books at our online bookstore, or enter our monthly scholarship contest. Don't get left in the dark when making your college decision. Let College Prowler be your guide!

Get the Jolt!

College Jolt gives you a peek behind the scenes

College Jolt is our new blog designed to hook you up with great information, funny videos, cool contests, awesome scholarship opportunities, and honest insight into who we are and what we're all about.

Check us out at **www.collegejolt.com**

COLLEGE PROWLER®

Need Help Paying For School?
Apply for our scholarship!

College Prowler awards thousands of dollars a year to students who compose the best essays. E-mail scholarship@collegeprowler.com for more information, or call 1-800-290-2682.

Apply now at **www.collegeprowler.com**

COLLEGE PROWLER®

Tell Us What Life Is Really Like at Your School!

Have you ever wanted to let people know what your college is really like? Now's your chance to help millions of high school students choose the right college.

Let your voice be heard.

Check out *www.collegeprowler.com* for more info!

Need More Help?

Do you have more questions about this school? Can't find a certain statistic? College Prowler is here to help. We are the best source of college information out there. We have a network of thousands of students who can get the latest information on any school to you ASAP. E-mail us at info@collegeprowler.com with your college-related questions.

E-Mail Us Your College-Related Questions!

Check out *www.collegeprowler.com* for more details.
1-800-290-2682

COLLEGE PROWLER®

Write For Us!
Get published! Voice your opinion.

Writing a College Prowler guidebook is both fun and rewarding; our open-ended format allows your own creativity free reign. Our writers have been featured in national newspapers and have seen their names in bookstores across the country. Now is your chance to break into the publishing industry with one of the country's fastest-growing publishers!

Apply now at **www.collegeprowler.com**

Contact editor@collegeprowler.com or call 1-800-290-2682 for more details.

COLLEGE PROWLER®

Pros and Cons

Still can't figure out if this is the right school for you? You've already read through this in-depth guide; why not list the pros and cons? It will really help with narrowing down your decision and determining whether or not this school is right for you.

Pros	Cons
....	....
....	....
....	....
....	....
....	....
....	....
....	....
....	....
....	....
....	....
....	....
....	....
....	....
....	....

COLLEGE PROWLER®

Pros and Cons

Still can't figure out if this is the right school for you?
You've already read through this in-depth guide;
why not list the pros and cons? It will really help
with narrowing down your decision and determining
whether or not this school is right for you.

Pros	Cons
....	....
....	....
....	....
....	....
....	....
....	....
....	....
....	....
....	....
....	....
....	....
....	....
....	....

COLLEGE PROWLER®

Notes

Notes

Notes

Notes

Notes

Notes

Notes

Notes

Notes

Notes

COLLEGE PROWLER®

Order now! • **collegeprowler.com** • 1.800.290.2682
Over 260 single-school guidebooks!

Albion College	Franklin & Marshall College	Ohio State University	University of Colorado
Alfred University	Furman University	Ohio University	University of Connecticut
Allegheny College	Geneva College	Ohio Wesleyan University	University of Delaware
American University	George Washington University	Old Dominion University	University of Denver
Amherst College	Georgetown University	Penn State University	University of Florida
Arizona State University	Georgia Tech	Pepperdine University	University of Georgia
Auburn University	Gettysburg College	Pitzer College	University of Illinois
Babson College	Gonzaga University	Pomona College	University of Iowa
Ball State University	Goucher College	Princeton University	University of Kansas
Bard College	Grinnell College	Providence College	University of Kentucky
Barnard College	Grove City College	Purdue University	University of Maine
Bates College	Guilford College	Reed College	University of Maryland
Baylor University	Gustavus Adolphus College	Rensselaer Polytechnic Institute	University of Massachusetts
Beloit College	Hamilton College	Rhode Island School of Design	University of Miami
Bentley College	Hampshire College	Rhodes College	University of Michigan
Binghamton University	Hampton University	Rice University	University of Minnesota
Birmingham Southern College	Hanover College	Rochester Institute of Technology	University of Mississippi
Boston College	Harvard University	Rollins College	University of Missouri
Boston University	Harvey Mudd College	Rutgers University	University of Nebraska
Bowdoin College	Haverford College	San Diego State University	University of New Hampshire
Brandeis University	Hofstra University	Santa Clara University	University of North Carolina
Brigham Young University	Hollins University	Sarah Lawrence College	University of Notre Dame
Brown University	Howard University	Scripps College	University of Oklahoma
Bryn Mawr College	Idaho State University	Seattle University	University of Oregon
Bucknell University	Illinois State University	Seton Hall University	University of Pennsylvania
Cal Poly	Illinois Wesleyan University	Simmons College	University of Pittsburgh
Cal Poly Pomona	Indiana University	Skidmore College	University of Puget Sound
Cal State Northridge	Iowa State University	Slippery Rock	University of Rhode Island
Cal State Sacramento	Ithaca College	Smith College	University of Richmond
Caltech	IUPUI	Southern Methodist University	University of Rochester
Carleton College	James Madison University	Southwestern University	University of San Diego
Carnegie Mellon University	Johns Hopkins University	Spelman College	University of San Francisco
Case Western Reserve	Juniata College	St. Joseph's University Philadelphia	University of South Carolina
Centenary College of Louisiana	Kansas State	St. John's University	University of South Dakota
Centre College	Kent State University	St. Louis University	University of South Florida
Claremont McKenna College	Kenyon College	St. Olaf College	University of Southern California
Clark Atlanta University	Lafayette College	Stanford University	University of Tennessee
Clark University	LaRoche College	Stetson University	University of Texas
Clemson University	Lawrence University	Stony Brook University	University of Utah
Colby College	Lehigh University	Susquehanna University	University of Vermont
Colgate University	Lewis & Clark College	Swarthmore College	University of Virginia
College of Charleston	Louisiana State University	Syracuse University	University of Washington
College of the Holy Cross	Loyola College in Maryland	Temple University	University of Wisconsin
College of William & Mary	Loyola Marymount University	Tennessee State University	UNLV
College of Wooster	Loyola University Chicago	Texas A & M University	Ursinus College
Colorado College	Loyola University New Orleans	Texas Christian University	Valparaiso University
Columbia University	Macalester College	Towson University	Vanderbilt University
Connecticut College	Marlboro College	Trinity College Connecticut	Vassar College
Cornell University	Marquette University	Trinity University Texas	Villanova University
Creighton University	McGill University	Truman State	Virginia Tech
CUNY Hunters College	Miami University of Ohio	Tufts University	Wake Forest University
Dartmouth College	Michigan State University	Tulane University	Warren Wilson College
Davidson College	Middle Tennessee State	UC Berkeley	Washington and Lee University
Denison University	Middlebury College	UC Davis	Washington University in St. Louis
DePauw University	Millsaps College	UC Irvine	Wellesley College
Dickinson College	MIT	UC Riverside	Wesleyan University
Drexel University	Montana State University	UC San Diego	West Point
Duke University	Mount Holyoke College	UC Santa Barbara	West Virginia University
Duquesne University	Muhlenberg College	UC Santa Cruz	Wheaton College IL
Earlham College	New York University	UCLA	Wheaton College MA
East Carolina University	North Carolina State	Union College	Whitman College
Elon University	Northeastern University	University at Albany	Wilkes University
Emerson College	Northern Arizona University	University at Buffalo	Williams College
Emory University	Northern Illinois University	University of Alabama	Xavier University
FIT	Northwestern University	University of Arizona	Yale University
Florida State University	Oberlin College	University of Central Florida	
Fordham University	Occidental College	University of Chicago	

Made in the USA
Lexington, KY
12 July 2010